MANUAL

OF

TELEGRAPHY

DESIGNED FOR BEGINNERS.

BY PROF. J. E. SMITH.

FOURTEENTH EDITION.

Published by L. G. TILLOTSON & CO.,
MANUFACTURERS OF AND DEALERS IN
Telegraph Instruments and Materia
OF EVERY DESCRIPTION,
5 & 7 DEY STREET,
NEW YORK.

PRICE, 30 CENTS PER COPY.

INTRODUCTORY

TO

SMITH'S MANUAL.

A SIMPLE DESCRIPTION OF THE MORSE SYSTEM OF TELEGRAPHY, PARTICULARLY ADAPTED FOR SELF INSTRUCTION IN THE ART.

The extensive increase in the practical use of Telegraphs in connection with many branches of business has made Telegraphy almost a necessary part of a business education even for those who do not expect to practice for a livelihood this most interesting and pleasant occupation.

Many of the more prominent manufacturers now find it to be not only a great convenience, but, in fact, an absolute necessity, to have a telegraph between the business office or salesroom and the factory.

The case is the same wherever there are two or more departments of the same business located at a distance from each other and requiring frequent communication.

The Bookkeeper, Clerk or Salesman who can add to his other acquirements a knowledge of Telegraphy will frequently find this knowledge useful to his employers as well as valuable to himself.

From the simplicity and peculiarly interesting nature of the pursuit, it proves to be neither tedious nor difficult to learn—the practice being more of a pleasant pastime than a labor, while a fair degree of skill may be acquired in a very short time.

One of the best plans by which a number of persons at a time may practice and learn Telegraphy *at home* is to connect, by a wire and instruments, several different residences situated either adjacently or at a distance from each other.

In this way neighbors and friends may jointly own a wire to which there is attached an instrument in each house, placing them all in electrical communication with each other for conversation by telegraph or for practice at learning Telegraphy.

The cost of such lines is exceedingly moderate—a mile of suitable wire and thirty-five insulators costing about $27.00, while the aggregate cost of the Batteries and instruments will average about ten dollars for each instrument connected. Beyond these amounts, the labor of putting up the wire (and erecting poles where there are neither trees nor buildings on which to fasten the wire) is the only additional expense of a complete working line.

This estimate applies as well to *all* short lines which are put up to serve purposes of convenient communication or for practice. It is the object of this work to furnish all information necessary to enable the amateur telegrapher to build and operate a line of telegraph as well as to understand the principles upon which the Electric Telegraph is based.

The Battery being the first essential part of the entire apparatus, the study should here begin.

It is from the action created in the Battery that is first generated the electric current, which, in practical Telegraphy, is made to traverse long or short distances through the conducting medium of metallic wires, and this current of electricity, so generated in the Battery, and so conducted through the wires, is then, by means of the proper instruments, which are herein described, made to give out tangible signals, which, being arranged in the form of an alphabet, enables us to read or speak as it were from any distance, by this means, instantaneously; for the electric current requires but a small fraction of a second's time to travel many hundreds of miles through the wires.

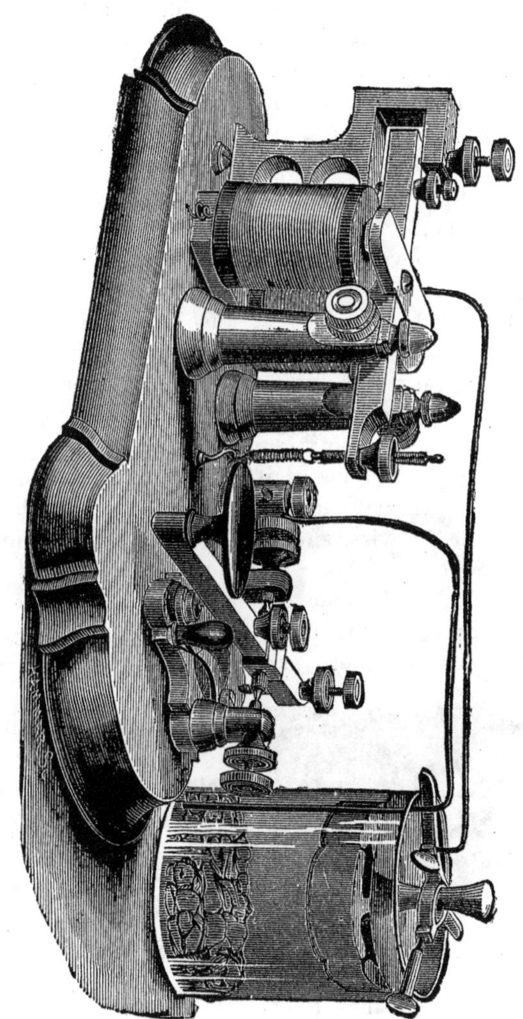

MORSE TELEGRAPH APPARATUS.

(*Key Sounder and Battery.*)

CONNECTED FOR OPERATION.

With the cut of the apparatus on the preceding page is represented one cell of Gravity Battery of the kind now most generally used for telegraphic purposes throughout the United States. It consists of a glass jar, about seven inches high, nearly filled with water, immersed in which at the bottom is a cross-form plate of copper, having fastened to it an insulated conducting wire, which, passing out at the upper part of the jar, constitutes what is termed the "copper" or "positive pole" of the Battery. Around and on the copper in the bottom of the jar are placed a few ounces of sulphate of copper.

Suspended above (by means of a brass tripod, or "hanger," as it is called), is a wheel of zinc, the body of which is allowed to remain beneath the surface of the liquid in the jar. The brass hanger is made to serve as a conductor from the zinc by means of a connecting post and screw for the attachment of a wire to one of its arms. This constitutes the negative or zinc pole of the Battery. Now, if the wire projecting upward from the copper be connected with the zinc, by attaching it at the screw-post on the hanger, a current of electricity will constantly flow from the copper to the zinc through the wire, and will cease to flow the moment the wire is disconnected. If the wire from the copper is made a mile in length, and its end connected in the same manner with the zinc, the current will flow through its entire length and come back to the zinc, just as surely as though the distance were but a few inches, and will instantaneously cease to flow the moment the wire is disconnected or broken at any point in its entire length.

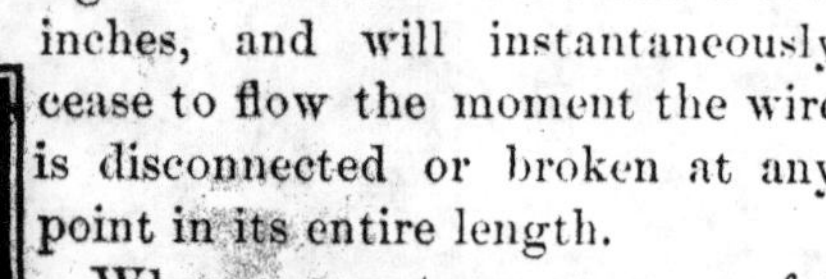

Where currents more powerful than can be produced by a single cell are required, additional cells are added, by connecting either the copper or zinc pole of the first cell to the opposite pole of the next, and so on; so that in a series of fifteen or twenty cells, if the unconnected pole of the cell at one end was copper, that pole would constitute the copper pole of the entire Battery, and the unconnected zinc at the other end would be the zinc pole of the entire Battery. By connecting the end of a wire of any length to the zinc or copper pole of such a Battery, and its opposite end to the remaining pole, a much more powerful current would pass through the wire than if the Battery consisted of but one cell. Telegraph companies, on their long lines, use Batteries of from twenty to one hundred cells each.*

TO PUT THE BATTERY IN OPERATION.

Fill the glass jar about two-thirds full of water; place the copper in the bottom so that it rests as nearly level as possible, and its wire passing straight upward at one side of the jar. Then drop about half a pound of sulphate of copper into the jar, so the lumps will lay evenly on the bottom or around and on the copper. Then suspend the zinc so that the body of the wheel is about two inches above the copper. As the Battery does not at once begin to act in its fullest strength when newly set up, it is well to connect the copper with the zinc and leave it so for a few hours before using. This is done by fastening the wire from the copper into the screw-post of the zinc hanger, and will soon cause the Battery to work up sufficiently to be ready for use. The Battery should be kept supplied with enough sulphate of copper so that a blue color can always be seen in the liquid at the bottom of the jar, rising to within an inch of the lower surface of the suspended zinc. If it is found that the blue color rises higher than this, it is thereby indicated too much sulphate of copper is being used, and no more should be put in until the blue has receded almost to the very bottom of the jar. The latter state of the Battery indicates that more sulphate of copper is required. Water should be from time to time added to that in the jar, to replace the loss by evaporation.

Once in two or three months it will be necessary to thoroughly clean the Battery. Take out the zinc carefully; then the copper in the same manner; pour the liquid into a separate jar, leaving behind the oxide and dirt which may have gathered in the bottom of the jar. Wash the latter out completely, and return to it the clean liquid which it had in it before; put back the copper to its place; put in a few crystals of sulphate of copper; clean the zinc thoroughly by scraping and washing, and return it also to its place. The Battery will then be in good order, and should not be disturbed

*See page 29, Smith's Manual.

excepting when necessary to clean it or add sulphate. The power of this Battery depends very much upon the position in which the zinc is placed with reference to the copper. To get the most active effect, lower the zinc to within about an inch of the copper, taking care not to allow a contact between the two. To decrease the power and render the Battery more constant or lasting, raise the zinc farther away from the copper.

CONDUCTORS AND INSULATION.*

Mention is made in the preceding chapter of the use of wire as the means of conducting currents of electricity from one pole of a Battery to any given point, and thence back to the opposite pole, making the "circuit," as it is called, complete. Certain substances are found to conduct electricity with more or less facility, and these substances are called conductors, while through other matter no currents whatever will pass. The latter class of substances are called non-conductors or insulating mediums.

In Telegraphy there are used as conductors, principally, copper, iron, brass, and platina. As insulation, gutta-percha, hard and soft rubber, glass, silk, and cotton fibre, dry wood, bone and ivory.

Iron in the shape of wire is usually employed for outside conductors, because of its durability, cheapness, and strength, although it is not as perfect a conductor as copper, which latter is generally used for all wires inside of buildings and offices.

In conducting currents of electricity from one point to another, as in Telegraphy, it is found necessary to use non-conductors wherever a fastening of the wire is made, in order to prevent escape of the fluid at these numerous points. For this purpose, glass is principally used for outside wires, the glass "insulators" being first made fast to the pole or building, whereon the wire is to be suspended, by means of a wooden pin,† or "bracket," after which the wire is strung, and tied to the glass with a short piece of iron "tie-wire." Inside of offices, hard and soft rubber tubes are used where the wires pass through the windows, and the copper conducting wires are usually covered with a coating of gutta-percha, or wrapped with a continuous covering of cotton or silk. The latter is principally used as a covering for the wires inside the finer in-

*See page 27, Smith's Manual.

†See page 29, Smith's Manual.

struments. For the handles or knobs to the various instruments which require manipulation, hard rubber is generally used.

THE EARTH AS A CONDUCTOR.

It is found that when one pole of a Battery is connected with the earth, and the wire from the opposite pole carried to a point at any distance away, and also connected with the earth, the current will flow as readily as though the "circuit" had been made complete by the use of a return wire. It is therefore shown that the earth is practically one vast conductor. This is principally due to the fact that moisture is everywhere present beneath the surface of the earth, and water itself is known to be a very fair conductor.

Telegraph companies make great practical use of earth conduction by using it in all cases for their numerous lines, both long and short, thus saving the construction of a separate or return wire on every circuit.

MAGNETS AND KEYS.*

A careful reading of the foregoing will have enabled the student to understand how currents of electricity are generated and made to travel through space. The next feature of the study will be the means which are employed to make these currents transmit signals.

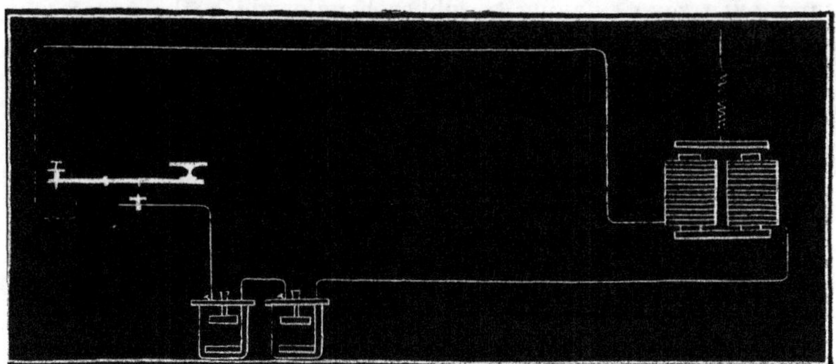

The basis of the entire Telegraphic apparatus is the electro-magnet and the transmitting "key." The electro-magnet is constructed as follows: Two bars of soft iron, having round heads of rubber or

*See pages 32 and 33, Smith's Manual.

wood, thus making spools of each, are fastened together by means of a short, flat bar of iron similarly soft. The round bars in the spools of the magnet are called the "cores." The flat connecting bar at the back is called the "back armature," by Telegraphers, to distinguish it from the movable piece in front, which is to be attracted to the "cores," or withdrawn by the spring, and which is called the armature.

A silk or cotton-covered wire is wound in continuous turns about the cores, until a diameter of about an inch and a half is attained, and each core or spool of the magnet contains a great number of turns of the wire around it. Now, if a current of electricity be sent through this wire, it will, by its passing through the numerous turns, cause the iron cores within to become magnetic and to possess the power of attracting with considerable force any piece of iron brought near to their ends. The cores, being made of soft iron, will lose their magnetism and cease to exert any attractive power, the moment the current ceases to flow. The actual power of the attractive force thus exerted is directly dependent upon the power of the Battery which supplies the current, or, more properly speaking, upon the power of the current itself. Strong currents will cause the magnets to attract with a power of several pounds.

*Keys are simply a contrivance for making or breaking the contacts which control the passage of the current—a brass lever, swung on a pivot, having a rubber handle which the operator grasps lightly with the thumb and fore-fingers. On pressing the lever downward, a platina point projecting under the lever is brought into contact with another platina point set into an insulation of rubber in the base of the key, so that there can be no electrical connection between them unless the key is pressed down, or "closed," as it is termed. A conducting wire being separated at any point, and one of its ends connected with the lever or base of the key, and the other end with the metal set into the rubber insulation, would convey the current while the key was closed, and cease to do so the moment it was opened. Platina is used at the points where the electrical contacts are made and broken, because it does not readily fuse or tarnish. An extra lever at the side of the key is called the "circuit-breaker," and is used as a means of

*See page 34, Smith's Manual.

keeping the circuit closed when the hand of the operator is not on the key. When the circuit-breaker is pushed into its closed position, it makes contact with a brass lip, which latter is fastened to the rubber along with the lower platina point. This, then, has the same effect as though the key was pressed downward and contact made at the points.

The cut on page vii represents a magnet with its armature suspended from a spring, and connected with it by a wire, a battery and a key. From what has now been explained, it may be seen that when the key is closed a current from the Battery will pass through the wire and magnet, and cause the latter to attract the armature, overcoming the resistance of the spring, and that the instant the key is opened the current will cease to flow, the magnet cease to attract, and the spring will instantly draw the armature back to its original position. In this way the armature is made to follow exactly the movements of the key, no matter at what distance they may be placed from each other, although in practice it is found that as the circuits are lengthened, more Battery power and more delicate instruments are required than on short lines.

The whole basis of the Telegraph system is this duplication at one point, by the magnet and its armature, of the motions made on the key by the hand of the operator, at another separate and distant point.

During the first years of Telegraphy, the Morse Register was the only means employed to put into tangible form the signals transmitted over the wires.

The cut on page 51 represents a working instrument of this kind, such as are now used in telegraph offices where all or a portion of the operators employed are not able to read by sound. And on page 48 will be found the code of signals already spoken of, and which are known as the Morse Alphabet.

In order to give the clearest possible idea of the operation of a Register, by which it records these signals, reference is made to the next paragraph, containing an outline diagram of the main working parts of the instrument and an accompanying explanation.

MORSE ALPHABET AND REGISTER.

The armature of the magnet is attached to a lever, and this lever, which swings on a pivot in the middle, is provided at the end with a pointed pin or screw, which is caused to press upwards against a strip of paper whenever the magnet attracts, and to return to its former position when the reverse is the case. Meanwhile the paper is kept moving steadily forward, so that if the lever-pin is pressed against the paper, for only an instant of time,

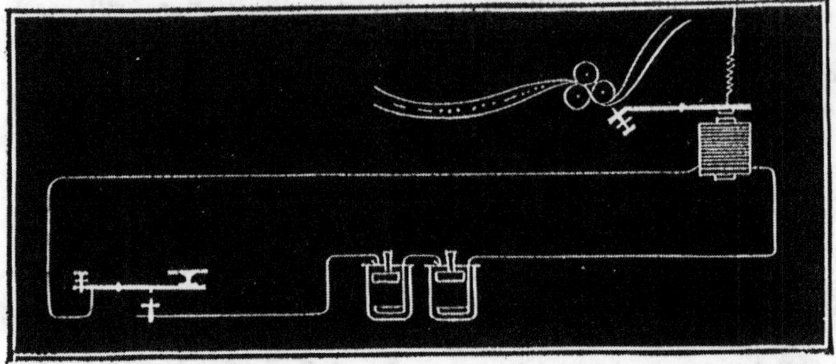

a short mark or *dot* appears pressed or embossed into the paper. If for a longer time, the mark would be proportionately longer, or a *dash.* If alternately, the marks would come consecutively, and have *spaces* between them. As the Morse Alphabet consists entirely of dots, dashes, spaces, and extra long dashes, the letters and numerals are easily made with these marks and their combinations. So that as the hand of the operator, on the key at a distant point, makes short or long strokes, dots, or dashes, or spaces, these same marks appear on the paper as it comes from the Register, and being based on the formation given by the Morse Alphabet, are as easily understood by the receiving operator as though they appeared in the well-known Roman characters.

After the Telegraph had been in successful operation for several years, the operators began to discover that, with practice, they could more easily distinguish the dots and dashes by the clicking sounds that came from the instrument, when the lever responded to the signals, than they could read them from the paper. This was the beginning of what is called READING BY SOUND. At the present time none are considered good operators who cannot read by sound, and there are comparatively few Registers in use in the United States.

TO SET UP THE INSTRUMENT FOR PRACTICE.

Having set up the Battery according to directions on page v, connect, as shown in the cut, one wire from the copper pole of the Battery to one of the brass binding-posts of the instrument, and one wire from the zinc pole to the remaining binding-post; screw down the instrument firmly to the table with the screw in the base, as its best sound is thereby produced. See that none of the screws are loose in their places, and that the armature lever, which is the speaking tongue of the Telegraph, plays freely, with a movement of about one-sixteenth of an inch. The spring, which draws the armature lever upwards, and is called the adjustment, should only be set at sufficient tension to raise the lever when no current is passing through the magnets. If drawn too tightly, the spring will not allow the armature to respond to the attractions of the magnet. When the instrument is not in use, leave the circuit-breaker of the key open so that the Battery will not be in action, and its power accordingly economized. See that the platina points of the key are kept clean from dirt or dust, thus preventing imperfect contacts from being made.

The key is provided with screws for the purpose of regulating its play to suit the hand of the operator, and to regulate also the pressure of the spring beneath it, for the same purpose.

A little practice will enable the student to judge best for himself as to how this should be set.

The best way to acquire the habit of correct Morse writing in the start, is by practicing with another student at the same instrument, one at making letters, while the other, by listening, endeavors to name them. This is excellent practice for both; it is the beginning of sound-reading on the part of the one who names the letters, while the one who writes on the key *must* make the signals distinctly and correctly, or they cannot possibly be distinguished by the other. Start rightly, and practice will soon make perfection of skill. No mental effort whatever is required of the practical operator to construct a Morse letter the moment his eyes come to it. And in transmitting messages he transmits the right signals in a continuous stream with as little effort or thought as the accomplished penman rapidly writes the words of a manuscript. The click of an instrument is as easily understood by a "sound operator" who has had an experience of a year or two, as his own language spoken in the clearest of accents.

After two or three weeks of practice together over one instrument, two persons should be able to read each other's writing slowly, and should also have become familiar with the instruments, Battery, and the principles of their operation. Separate practice over a short line between different rooms or buildings may then with advantage begin, each student having an instrument connected at his own end of the wire, and all communication between them necessarily being made by telegraph. According to the length of line between the two instruments, two or more cells of Battery, arranged in series, as described on page iv, will be required to operate in this way. Connect instruments and Battery as follows:

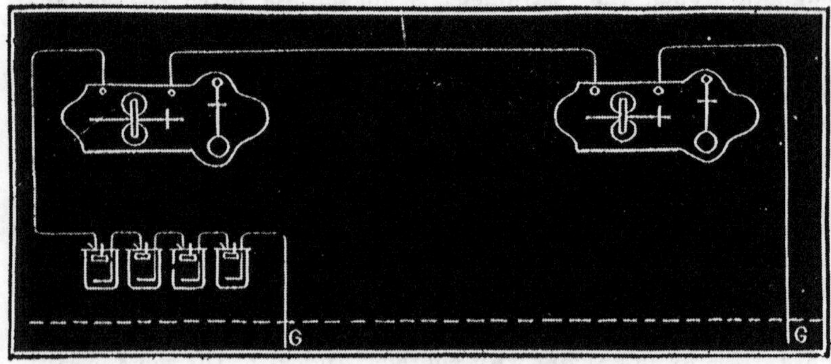

The return circuit may be made either by a continuous wire, as indicated, or by connection with the earth at each end, *G G*. For wires of but a short distance in length, the return wire is best;

for out-door lines of more than a few hundred feet in length, use ground-wires, as earth connections are called. To make a ground wire, connect a wire to a plate or sheet of metal, zinc, iron, or tin; bury the latter in moist earth. The plate of metal should present not less than three square feet of surface. Gas and water pipes are, however, the best for this attachment, and whenever they are within reach should be used instead of buried plates in the earth.

In running an out-door wire between points at any distance apart, it should be insulated (by using glass or rubber insulators) from all direct contact with buildings, posts, or trees.* This prevents "escape" of the current, by which it would otherwise be diverted from its proper course through both of the instruments, and reaching the earth by a shorter route, would circulate to its opposite pole in the Battery without having any effect whatever on the distant apparatus. To make a joint or splice in wire, brighten the ends by scraping them, and twist each wire around the other as closely and firmly as possible, so that no strain will draw them apart.*

In running wires inside of a building, use insulated copper wire covered either with cotton or gutta-percha; fasten it in place with small staples or tacks, but in doing so be careful not to allow the covering to be opened or stripped from the wire, nor to allow the latter to come in contact with gas or water pipes, or metal posts.

In the beginning, when two persons are first practicing over a short wire, arranged as described, ordinary conversation carried on by Telegraph is as good a means of practice, both at sending and at reading, as anything else. Then proceed with alternately sending printed matter from newspapers or books and copying it with a pen or pencil from the instrument by sound as the other sends it. As each improves, both in reading by sound and in sending plainly, this will become very pleasant and interesting occupation.

It is often desired to connect three or more instruments or "offices" in the same wire, each office being in a different locality.

*See pages 28 and 29, Smith's Manual.

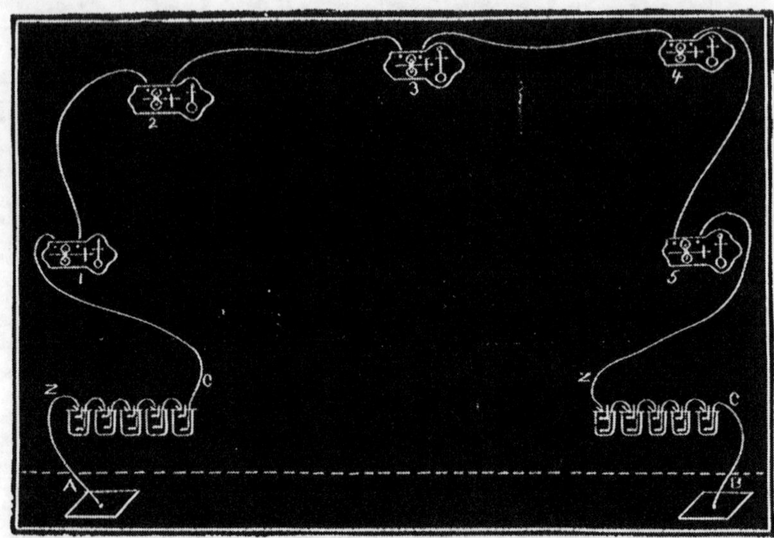

The above diagram illustrates the manner of connecting wires, instruments and Batteries, on such a line, batteries being placed at each end of the wire. Battery at A has its zinc pole connected to the earth and its copper to the line; necessarily therefore the other Battery at B presents its zinc pole to the line and its copper to the earth. If both Batteries were connected with the same pole to the line, they would neutralize each other and no current whatever would be produced.

The line is connected as shown from the Battery to the first instrument and on to the next in such a way that the current is made to pass through each and every instrument on the route.

Each office should have a call or signal for itself.* Any one or two letters of the alphabet will suit, and serves in working over the line as the name of whatever office it is applied to. One office desiring to communicate with another, writes on the line the call of that office, three or four times, followed by his own call, and repeats this operation indefinitely, or until he is answered by the office calling. The office answering the call makes the letter "I" three or four times and signs his own call. The receipt of a communica-

*See page 22, Smith's Manual.

tion is answered by the signal "O K," followed by the signal or call of the office receiving it. If the receiver, from any cause, fails to read or understand any portion of the communication, he calls for a repetition by "breaking-in" and saying "G A" (go ahead from), and giving the last word understood by him. If he wishes it repeated entirely, he says "R R" (repeat).

It is necessary where two or more offices are connected together on a line, that every key should be kept closed by having its circuit-breaker shut, excepting only while sending communications. If any one key on the entire line is left open, all communication is stopped. The reason for this has already been fully explained.

As lightning is frequently attracted to out-door lines, and thereby enters the offices, sometimes damaging the instruments or even setting fire to curtains or other inflammable material about the instrument table, a simple and cheap instrument, called "lightning arrester and cut-out," is used for the purpose of intercepting and carrying to the earth such discharges of lightning as would be liable to cause damage. This apparatus is entirely effective, and is a complete safeguard against lightning.

When several persons are jointly practicing on a line in which there are a number of separate instruments, placed either in different rooms or in different houses, all are thus in communication with each other, and while any one of them is writing, all the rest can simultaneously practice at reading by sound.

Main lines of Telegraph are arranged in precisely the same way. With wires of many miles in length, main Batteries, containing a large number of cells, are placed at the end stations. The return circuit is made through the earth the entire distance, and each office connected to the line in the manner here described. The means employed to "tap" a Telegraph line (which is sometimes done in case of railway accidents and for other purposes), are very simple, and will serve to illustrate this. The wire is simply cut, and its two ends connected to a portable instrument in the hands of a "sound-operator," who may then easily read all that passes over the wire.

PRACTICAL DIRECTIONS.

The question is often asked, "How much Battery or how many cells, and what kind of Battery will work a certain length of line to which are connected a certain number of instruments?"

The Gravity Battery (see catalogue,) described herein, is the adopted standard form in general use by most companies, and is considered to be the best for all ordinary purposes. For short lines, etc., its proper use may be practically set down according to the proportions given below; bearing in mind, however, that the greater the number of cells of Battery used, the more powerfully the instruments will work, and that if it is found when one or more instruments are properly connected in a circuit according to directions, it or they do not work with enough strength to give the amount of sound wanted, addition of more Battery will produce better results.

For one instrument, use one or two cells of Gravity Battery. For two instruments in connection, not farther than 100 feet apart, two or three cells, adding one cell for each additional instrument connected to the same wire; also add further one cell for each quarter of a mile added to the length of the wire up to one mile, and then two or three cells for each additional mile.

For such lines, "No. 12 Galvanized iron" is the least expensive wire suitable for the purpose. For lines of between one and twelve miles in length, the instruments are required to have their magnets wound with finer wires than those used on circuits of less than one mile. Such instruments are designated as being of "20 ohms resistance." This fact should be remembered when ordering equipments for a line of over one and under twelve miles long.

Never use in the same line instruments of different resistance. Whatever other differences there may be in the instruments, they should be all alike in resistance.

For more complete description of Morse Telegraphs as they are at present operated, the student is now referred to Smith's Manual of Telegraphy, Part II.

In Part I. will be found all the necessary rudimentary exercises and instruction which pertains to the practical acquirement of skill in Morse writing and reading, together with forms of messages, manner of communicating over a wire, abbreviations used, etc.

INTRODUCTORY REMARKS.

Although the principal design of this work is to instruct in the art of *reading by sound*, yet those who desire to acquire the faculty of reading from paper will find the instructions equally well suited to their wants, it being impossible to give directions adapted to sound reading which are not applicable to reading by sight; indeed, every one pursuing the latter method is, in reality, governed quite as much by the clicks of the register as by the impression which it makes.

The system of instruction adopted in the first part is the result of close and long continued observation. It not only tells the student precisely *how* to proceed in the formation of nearly every character, but, in showing the right way, depends much on pointing out to him *where* and *how* he is likely to fail. Like observation has also made it clear that the Morse characters should never be placed before the student in alphabetical order. This part is intended to be practiced and mastered as fast as read.

The second part, in setting forth the construction of a telegraph line, and the principles on which it is operated, although drawing to some extent on the imagination, aims to instruct synthetically, by commencing with the fundamental principles of electro-magnets, and explaining addition after addition until a full line is pictured, as well as the various obstacles arising to impede or interrupt its workings. History and theory are entirely discarded, the present condition of the telegraph and the known principles on which its working depends being all that is valuable to the student. This portion may be studied in connection with the writing exercises, and it should be reviewed a number of times.

While it is believed that the student, in following the line of instruction as herein laid before him, will progress more rapidly than by the adoption of any other mode of procedure, he is warned against falling into the too common error of expecting great results from little labor. There is no duty of a telegraphist which any person of ordinary ability may not readily learn to perform, if he will but bestow the attention which he should willingly give to any undertaking. Students with a clear understanding of the customs and principles set forth in these instructions, and able to copy each other's telegraphic writing by sound at the rate of thirty-five words per minute, may consider themselves *operators*.

PART I.

INSTRUCTIONS IN MANIPULATION AND BUSINESS FORMS.

MORSE CHARACTERS.

L or cypher	T	E	I	S	H	P	6	A
—	-	.	..	...	....	.....	......	.-

U	V	4	N	D	B	8	G
..-	...-	....-	-.	-..	-...	-....	--.

7	Exclamation	F	Comma	Semicolon	Quotation
--..	---.	.-.	.-.-	.--.--	.---.--.-

X	W	1	Parenthesis	Q	2
.-..	.--	.--.	.----	..-.	..--.

Period	3	M	5	Paragraph	Interrogation
..--..	...-.	--	.---	----	-..-.

Italics	9	K	J	O	R	&
-...-	-..-	-.-	-.-.	. .	. ..	. ...

C	Z	Y
.. .	... .	.. ..

These characters, forty-five in number, are formed of three simple elementary marks; the dot, the short dash, and the long dash. These elements, uncombined, are respectively E, T, and L or cipher. The remaining forty-two are made up of the dot and the short dash, the long dash never being used in combination, nor repeated except to repeat the letter or figure which it represents. The original intention was to use a longer dash for the cipher than for the letter L, but practice has made no difference in them, the long dash being invariably translated according to its connection. As an initial, or when joined with letters, it is always L ; when found among figures it is necessarily a cipher.

Six of the symbols, C, O, R, Y, Z, and &, contains each a *space*, the shorter separation of the elements being denominated *breaks*. The latter are only long enough to make the elements distinct from one another : the former occupies about the room that do a dot and a break.

It is well for every operator to be familiar with all the characters in the preceding table, though some of the punctuation marks are not in general use, and on some lines hardly known. A careful examination of their formation is all that is necessary before commencing to practice them, as they can generally be committed to memory sooner than they can be made with the key.

Marks of quotation, parenthesis, or italics, are placed both before or after the word or words affected by their use.

The main points to be acquired as a basis for the whole are embraced in the following six principles, which are to be mastered before any attempt is made to form other characters.

First principle,		Dots close together.
Second	"	Dashes close together.
Third	"	Lone dots.
Fourth	"	Lone dashes.
Fifth	"	A dot with a dash closely following.
Sixth	"	A dash closely followed by a dot.

POSITION AND MOVEMENT OF THE HAND.

Place the first two fingers on the top of the button to the key, with the thumb partly beneath it, thus forming a gentle grasp on the button. Let the fingers resting on it be considerably bent, so that the thumb will not slip from the under side, and the wrist and arm be entirely clear of the table. The wrist must be perfectly limber, and no stiffness should be given to any part of the hand. No exertion is to be made with the thumb and fingers other than in grasping the key, and from this they should not be permitted to fly during manipulation. They borrow their force from the hand and wrist, which should move directly up and down through a distance of about three-quarters of an inch. The motion, both up and down, must be *free* and *full*, and of moderate firmness. A large majority of students write with much too little force, and they are inclined to limit the amount of movement, holding the lever down when it should rise, and keeping it up when they should press it down.

Avoid the error of pressing down with the fingers while the wrist is thrown up, and *vice versa*. The wrist, hand, fingers, and key should move in the same direction.

Remembering that the downward movement produces sounds corresponding with dots and dashes, and the upward motion the sounds representing breaks and spaces, the student may proceed with the *first principle*, making a series of dots at the rate of four or five a second, or as fast as a detached lever watch ticks. No attempt to increase this speed should be made until the whole alphabet can be readily formed, when the rate can be gradually accelerated thirty or forty per cent. Fifty per cent. increase makes very rapid manipulation. Some will find it necessary to write even more moderately; and no one should manipulate more rapidly than he can do it well. The series of dots should be drilled on until the raps sound as regular as if made by clockwork.

The *second principle* may be started at the rate of one dash to a second of time, and slowly increased to three. Though uniformity in the acceleration of stroke is here desired, the important end to be obtained is a close proximity of the dashes—*breaks*, and not *spaces* being wanted between them. In this exercise the rule is to hold the lever down; the exception being to allow an upward *flash* of the hand, bringing the key down again in the shortest possible time. If the upward motion be *full*, it is impossible for the most rapid operator to make his marks, whether dots or dashes, too near each other, where a regular space is not required. It must be continually borne in mind that every character not containing a *space* must be *compact*, and not open and disjointed, so as to entirely change the meaning by a division of one character into two or more shorter ones.

In commencing the *third principle* the student will be assisted by the knowledge that nearly every first attempt at making a single dot produces a short dash. A quick but firm downward flash of the key will form a good letter E. The hand should no sooner start downward than it is quickly raised, as if the first movement were a mistake. This principle holds true in every case where a *space* follows a dot.

In drilling on this, or any other character, it should not be repeated too rapidly ; nor should the thumb and fingers be taken from the key during the short intervals, but through every space the thumb should pull up gently on the key ; during manipulation there must always be either an upward or a downward pressure exerted.

The *fourth principle*, T, L, and cipher, requires quite as much care as the letter E. An untrained hand sometimes makes T too short, but is rather inclined to the other extreme, especially when writing words ; and it, almost without exception, fails to make L, or cipher, of sufficient length ; indeed, both are so varied that in not a few cases students will be found making L shorter than T.

The time consumed in making the short dash is about equal to that occupied in pronouncing the word *tea*. For L, double the time must be given, or about one second. It had better be made much longer than is necessary than a little too short, for in the former case it cannot be misinterpreted.

A dot with a dash closely following, or the *fifth principle*, is executed by giving the key one flash and one moderately slow closing, the hand going with a bound from the dot to the dash. The pronunciation of the word *again*, with the second syllable strongly accented, furnishes very correct time for the letter A.

At the start, most every one finds himself inclined to make the dot too long and the dash too short, but more particularly to separate them too much.

The *sixth principle*, a dash closely followed by a dot, is one of the most difficult combinations. The tendency of the unpracticed to shorten the dash and lengthen the dot is so great that they are frequently reversed, forming A. This, however, can generally be remedied much sooner than they can be brought near enough together.

Measuring the time for the dash as correctly as possible, for the dot the hand must give a quick flash, as if it were trying to place the dot on top of the dash. The student must not think of taking his hand up from the dash before beginning the dot; that is, the downward position of the key is to be taken as the starting point of the dot.

A strict observance of this rule will alone prevent the occurrence of a space after the dash.

Timing by the pronunciation of the word *story*, dwelling on the first syllable rather longer than usual, and clipping the last very short, may prove to be good assistance. No more time should elapse between the dash and the dot than separates the two syllables of *story* in its pronunciation.

Justice having been done the six fundamental principles, the following exercises may be taken up in regular order, each character to be made many times before the next is practiced:

EXERCISE I.

E	I	S	H	P	6
-	- -	- - -	- - - -	- - - - -	- - - - - -

After practicing these separately until the right number of dots can be made and the last dot in each character as short as the others, run them forward and backward several times, making each one but once before proceeding to the next.

EXERCISE II.

A	U	V	4
·—	··—	···—	····—

In this exercise be particularly cautious to leave no space between the dots and the dash. This is the only error likely to be made. Let the dash follow the dots just as closely as if it were itself a dot.

It should be observed that this exercise is merely prolonging the last dot in I, S, H, and P.

EXERCISE III.

I	A	S	U	H	V	P	4
··	·—	···	··—	····	···—	·····	····—

These are to be produced in couples, as represented, but no letter is to be made twice in succession. The object is to make and readily detect the difference in those in the same couple on account of their similarity.

EXERCISE IV.

N	D	B	8
—·	—··	—···	—····

Directions for the formation of N have already been given. It is only necessary to remember that the dots must be started from the depressed position of the hand, and that the last dot in each must be made by a movement seemingly quicker than that required for the others.

EXERCISE V.

A	Comma	F	Semicolon	Quotation
·—	·—·—	·—·	·—·—·	·—·—·—·—
	X	W	1	Parenthesis
	·—··	·——	·——·	·—··—

Each of these, it will be seen, commences with A ; and care should be taken to begin them accordingly. The comma and quotation, being nothing more than A's close together, should be made without difficulty. F is probably as difficult as any character in this exercise. A and N must be thought of at nearly the same instant. It may be commenced with the dash much too long, in order to get the dots placed near enough to it, and then the dash may be gradually shortened until it becomes of proper length.

The semicolon can be referred to A and F, or comma and E closely united. X is likely to be separated into A I, or more frequently into E D.

In forming W and 1 care must not only be taken to have them compact, but to get the dashes of equal length. The general tendency is to make the last one too short, and not in these alone, but wherever two or more dashes occur together.

There seems to be no better rule for the parenthesis than to put A and U close together.

EXERCISE VI.

U	Q	2	Period	3
- - —	- - — -	- - — - -	- - —— - -	- - - — -

The warnings already given should make these characters comparatively easy, as they differ from some in Exercise V only in starting with a dot or two more. V and E, closely joined, will form 3 ; and U D will make a period when properly put together.

EXERCISE VII.

M	G	7	5	Exclamation
— —	— — -	— — - -	———	— — — -

Paragraph — — — —

The breaks in these, as made by the young operator, are seldom short enough, and the last dash, as before remarked, hardly long enough.

7 must not be turned into M I or M A, as is many times done.

EXERCISE VIII.

9	Interrogation	Italics	K	J
— - - —	— - - — -	— - - - —	— - —	— - — -

If any difficulty is experienced with 9, it should be formed from T U or D T, accordingly as the student may be oppositely inclined to divide it.

Any other guide seems unnecessary for the next two characters. J and K are generally more difficult of formation than any of the other characters, ninety-nine persons in one hundred insisting on dividing the one into double N, and the other into N T. K should always be practiced before J, and by closely following T with A, the movement for the latter being uppermost in the mind.

After the K motion is firmly fixed in the hand and mind, J may be produced by simply adding one dot, extreme caution being taken not to change the second dash into a dot and space, forming D E.

EXERCISE IX.

O	R	&	C	Z	Y
- -	- --	- ---	-- -	--- -	-- --

These can only be referred to E, I, and S, of which they are made. The spacing should be just sufficient to easily show that they are not intended for I, S and H. The tendency is to open them too much, or make a dash of the dot immediately preceding the space.

EXERCISE X.

When all the characters have been correctly made, according to the preceding exercises and accompanying directions, they may then be practiced in alphabetical order, but not before; for this reason they do not appear alphabetically anywhere in this book. The very common desire to begin making them in this order, and to write one's own name, even before the letters composing it have been tried separately, is altogether wrong, and should never be indulged in.

From this time onward the student should continually bear in mind that unless he is on the alert he will be making heavy dots just before spaces separating dots from dashes, but more especially dashes from dashes, and making T's too long and L's *much* too short. There are, however, certain combinations of letters in which some of these tendencies are reversed. Thus, a difficulty is found in getting the dash in 8 near the dots, and yet the same individual, in writing *th*, finds it too convenient to join them into the figure which he is inclined to separate. The same is true in regard to *an* and figure 1, *me* and G, N and *te*, D and *ti*. There is a strong inclination to join A, or a lone dot, to the last end of T and L, more particularly the latter.

Uniformity of space between letters, and between words also, is of no less importance than correct proportion of the letters themselves. The distance between two adjacent letters should be about great enough to accommodate one dot, though some operators place them still nearer. Double this space is to be left between words. A very common fault of young operators is to run their words too closely together—a fault which causes more trouble in reading than any other *one* feature of poor manipulation.

To the rule for spacing letters there are two exceptions:

Double E must contain a space nearly as great as that between words.

Double L, or two or more ciphers, need not be spaced, and they usually are not. If properly made they cannot be mistaken for anything else, as no character is formed of two or more long marks.

The words *let, tell, little, take, lake,* and *train* will furnish good exercise for overcoming some wrong and strong tendencies.

When more than three figures are used to express a whole number they should be divided into periods of three figures each, as in ordinary notation, the periods being spaced from each other the same as words. Thus: 1,250,095 in telegraphic writing will be

In fractions, one dot is made to represent the line between the numerator and the denominator.

1-2 is thus expressed:
7-8 " "
4 3-5 " "

No sign for dollars or cents is employed, consequently these words must be written out in full. Indeed, nothing can be telegraphed which cannot be spelled. Some private marks, as those used on boxes of goods, can, in substance, be transmitted by substituting for them words expressing their shape.

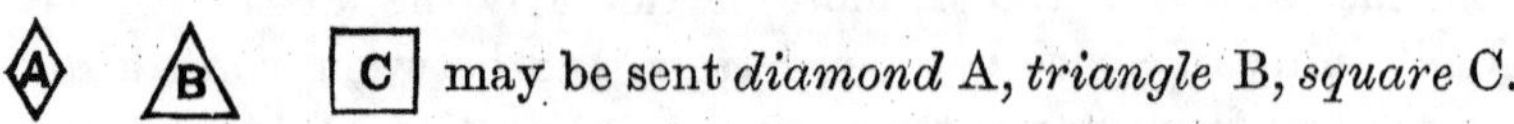

may be sent *diamond* A, *triangle* B, *square* C.

When the directions thus far have been thoroughly executed, and the figures have become as familiar as the letters, most any short words may be taken up and written without a copy to be looked at. In learning the telegraph, the fault of going over a great deal and doing nothing well is a universal one. In writing from memory less ground is likely to be poorly run over, and one learns to send and spell at the same time, which, at first, is rather difficult.

As one cannot learn to read by sound from his own writing, he always knowing what is intended to be made, two persons must practice together, taking turns at reading and writing, and each correcting the faults of the other.

At first the characters must be learned separately, then short words chosen and written slowly and very distinctly, and well spaced. It is impossible to give much instruction that will assist in recognizing the different sounds—but there is one point to be noted—the lever makes a sound at each movement, the downward motion producing a heavier one, or that representing dots and dashes ; or, more properly, the heavy stroke indicates the commencement of a dot or a dash, and the lighter sound shows when the mark ceases. E makes just as much noise as does L, the only difference being in the length of time between the heavy and the light sounds, L having no sound except at the ends. Then, if the recoil or lighter vibration be dispensed with, E, T, and L will all sound alike. Strict attention must be paid to this fact in all the letters having spaces in them, in order that they may not be confounded with the letters which they would form if the dot immediately preceding the space were changed to a dash, filling up the space.

Thus, compare well the sounds of O and N, R and D, C and F, & and B, Z and Q, Y and X.

MESSAGES.

The form of regular dispatches differs but little from that of letters. Each is first dated, then addressed to some party ; next comes the information to be communicated, followed by the name of the person writing it.

The terms applied to the different portions of a telegram are *date, address, body, signature,* and *check ;* and this is the order in which a dispatch is written and sent over a line.

The check is the number of words in the body of a message, and the price of transmission.

What the party sending the message says to the party addressed, or all that occurs between the address and the signature, constitutes the body ; and this alone is counted and charged for, unless there are more distinct signatures than one, in which case all but the last signature is counted. Any number of names, however, constituting one firm, is to be regarded as but one signature.

Telegrams should contain as few words as possible, and at the same time clearly convey the meaning intended. The use of

"Dear Sir," "Yours, &c.," is entirely unnecessary, and seldom indulged in, as they must be considered a part of the body of the message.

Notwithstanding the adoption by leading telegraph companies of certain rules for counting, there is not at the present time any uniformity in the reckoning of compound words. It was the design of these companies to have most compound words counted *one* word for the whole compound, but the customs of operators have made the exception a better guide than the rule.

To-day, to-night, and *to-morrow,* are each *one* word.

Except A. M. and P. M., meaning forenoon and afternoon (which are called one word each), every initial is counted a word. and F. O. B., C. O. D., signifying *free on board* and *collect on delivery,* are three words each. Custom has made two words of such numbers as twenty-six, forty-eight, seventy-two, &c., &c.

No abbreviations are permitted in the body of a message, and all numbers are first spelt out in full and afterward repeated in figures—the words, and not the figures, being counted.

When desired, a company will insure the correct transmission of a dispatch for a tariff fifty per cent. higher than the usual rate, in which case it is repeated back to the operator first sending it, and he compares the repetition with the original copy.

Some lines have also doubled their rates on a certain kind of commercial dispatch, called *cipher message.* The body of these is made up of disjointed words, apparently conveying no idea, and is intended to be understood only by the party addressed.

There is but one *method* of charging for messages, ten words always being the greatest number that can be sent for the least money. Any number less than ten, costs the same as ten, but each word in excess of that number is subject to a certain additional charge. The *rates* on different lines, and for different distances on the same line, vary; but the *system* of charging is precisely the same throughout this country.

If two or more copies of one dispatch are delivered to different parties, each copy must be paid for at the full rate.

Agents frequently send the same thing to five or six persons or firms.

The charges on a telegram going over any number of lines are *all* paid in advance or *all* collected on delivery. As dispatches themselves are valueless to a telegraph company, pre-payment is usually required ; but when it is known that the party addressed can be found and the charges collected of him, a message is sent *collect.*

CORRECT FORM OF ORDINARY TELEGRAMS.

BUFFALO, May 9th, 1865.

TO FISHER & HAMILTON,

New York.

Send thirty-five (35) gross, at seven three-eighths (7⅜) Funds to-morrow.

T. M. LONG.

10 75 Pd.

The operator sending has to insert the abbreviations "Fr." (from) and "Sig." (signature). With "Fr." he starts to write the dispatch, and at the end of the body "Sig." is introduced, as a warning to the operator receiving, that he may place the signature in its proper position. These *abbreviations, or the words they represent, are never copied by the receiver.*

The month and year of the date are never sent over the line, and sometimes the *day* of the month is not, when it is transmitted the same day on which it is written. If written or handed into the office a day or more before sent, the correct date is telegraphed.

When the party sending, requests the hour and minute of the date to be transmitted, the request is complied with.

A period should always be used at the end of the address, and at the close of every complete sentence, except just before the signature. It is never placed after initials, and no kind of punctuation is made use of, except at the end of the address and in the body of the dispatch.

Many operators punctuate only with the period, scarcely knowing the shorter pauses.

The foregoing message should therefore be thus written on the line.

- — -   -   - -   — - - -   - - —   - — -   - — -   - —   —   -   -

— - - —   —   - -   - — -   - -   - - -   - - - -   -   - - -

-   - - -   - - - -   - —   — —   - -   —   —   -   -   — -

— -   -   - — —   - -   - -   -   -   -   - -   — - —   - - — — - -

- - -   -   — -   — - -   —   - - - -   - -   -   - -   —   - -   - -

- — -   - -   - - - —   -   - - - — -   — — —   — — -   -   - -

-   - - - -   - - -   - —   —   - - -   -   - - — -   -   — -

—   - - - -   -   - -   -   -   -   - -   — — -   - - - -   —   - - - -

- - -   — — - -   - - - — -   -   — - - - -   - - — — - -

- — -   - - —   — -   — - -   - - -   —   -   -   — —   - -   -   - -

-   - -   - -   - — —   - - -   - -   — — -   —   — —

—   - -   — -   — — -   - — — -   —   — — - -

— — —   - - - - -   — - -

The check (Ck.) 10 75 Pd. (paid), signifies that there are ten words in the message, and that the price of transmission is 75 cents (the amount being always stated in cents), the abbreviation "Pd." showing that the dispatch is *prepaid*. "Col." accompanies some checks, indicating that the charges are to be collected of the party to whom the message is addressed.

When "Pa." is found in a check it is an order to pay out the amount following it, usually to a connecting line, but sometimes to the messenger for delivering the message some distance from the telegraph office.

There are several forms of checks having one signification, but that can be easily understood by remembering that the check of every dispatch which is *not prepaid* must contain the term *Col.*; and that the *absence* of *Col.* always determines prepayment, even if *Pd.* does not accompany the check.

In the following forms, all which appear in the same group are of like import:

CHECKS FOR PREPAID DISPATCHES GOING OVER BUT ONE COMPANY'S LINE.

10 50 10 50 Pd 10 Pd 50
10 N Y 50 Pd

The last form, in use on some lines, is to place before the amount the "call" of the office which receives the charges, whether prepaid or not, and after the amount to state if *Pd.* or *Col.* It will be seen that in this form the letters, both before and after the amount, decide the place of payment.

CHECKS FOR DISPATCHES GOING OVER BUT ONE LINE, AND TO BE PAID ON DELIVERY.

10 Col 50 10 50 Col 10 N Y 50 Col

CHECKS FOR MESSAGES GOING OVER TWO OR MORE LINES, AND INDICATING PREPAYMENT.

10 90 40 10 90 Pa 40
10 Pd 90 Pa 40 10 N Y 50 & 40 Pd

Each of these four forms means that 90 is the total charge, 50 of it belonging to the first company and 40 to the connecting line.

CHECKS FOR DISPATCHES GOING OVER TWO OR MORE LINES, CHARGES TO BE PAID AT THE DESTINATION.

10 Col 90 Pd 40 10 N Y Col 90 Pd 40
10 N Y 50 & 40 Col

These forms show that the company delivering the message collects of the address 90, keeps 50 of it, and pays 40 to the line connecting with it.

When a dispatch goes over several lines, and is prepaid, two amounts are used in the check until it passes over the last line, when it is reduced to its simplest form—one amount: when *collect* over a number of lines, one amount is used in the first check, and two amounts in all of the rest.

The form 10 90 Pa 40 orders to be paid to the next line all that does not belong to the line sending. Thus if a message of 10 words goes over four different lines, the charge on each of which is 25, the check will be on the

First line, 10 100 Pa 75
Second " 10 75 Pa 50
Third " 10 50 Pa 25
Fourth " 10 25

In using the form 10 N Y 50 & 40 Pd, each line keeps its own rate separate in the first amount, the second being the tariff for the remainder of the route, whether one or several companies.

Thus, for four lines, each charging 25, we have:

First line, 10 A 25 & 75 Pd
Second " 10 B 25 & 50 Pd
Third " 10 C 25 & 25 Pd
Fourth " 10 D 25 Pd

The first form of check for a *collect* message going over four lines at 25 cents each, gives:

First line 10 Col 25
Second " 10 Col 50 Pd 25
Third " 10 Col 75 Pd 50
Fourth " 10 Col 100 Pd 75

The last style, under like circumstances, produces:

First line, 10 A 25 Col
Second " 10 B 25 & 25 Col
Third " 10 C 25 & 50 Col
Fourth " 10 D 25 & 75 Col

The first company sending a *collect* message receives its charges from the second company; the second collects from the third the rate of the first added to its own; from the fourth the third receives the charges over the first three lines, and so on, until the last company, on delivering the message, collects from the party addressed the full amount for transmission.

On a *free* message, in place of the check, is sent "D H," signifying "Dead Head," or *no charge.* Sometimes the number of words in D H messages is sent the same as in paid dispatches; but in many instances, as on railroad lines, where it is well understood what communications should be *free*, even the D H is omitted.

FORM OF CIPHER DISPATCH, AS USED ON MILITARY TELEGRAPHS, OR BY SPECULATORS, TO RENDER IT UNINTELLIGIBLE TO ALL EXCEPT THE PARTY ADDRESSED.

To Brown, Henderson & Co.,
Hartford, Ct.

Aloud rampant honor deal boots bang bag cut order fox.
10 30 Pd

FORM OF DISPATCHES BETWEEN OFFICES CORRECTING ERRORS, OR MAKING INQUIRIES RELATING TO THE BUSINESS OF THE LINE.

These are known as *Ofs* (office) *messages*, and are, of course, D H.

To Chicago Ofs.

Can't find Hawley & Jones, 25 Fulton St., message 18th, signed Peterson. Give better address.

New York Ofs.

REPLY.

To New York Ofs.

Find Hawley & Jones, 75 Fulton St. not 25. Hurry answer.

Chicago Ofs.

To understand more particularly the method of sending and receiving dispatches, it must be known that every office has a *call*, which is usually one or two of the letters occurring in the name of the place, but in a few instances a letter not to be found in the name, or a figure, is used. The calls are the signals made use of in arresting the attention of the different stations, as desired ; therefore, all offices on the same line, or at least all that communicate direct, one with another, must have different signals. Operators must in all cases be able to distinguish their own *calls* by sound.

One office desiring to communicate with another, makes the call of that station three or four times, then gives his own office signal, and keeps repeating this until he receives a reply, or gets tired of calling.

An office answering a call makes the letter I two or three times, more or less, then its own call.

An acknowledgment of the receipt of any kind of communication is made by returning O K, followed by the call of the office receiving the communication.

Writing one's own office call is termed *signing ;* and this must be done *once* and *only* once, at the close of everything that is written over a line, be it calling, answering calls, giving O K, sending messages, or conversing.

Let N Y be the call for New York, and B that for Boston, and the New York operator will call the attention of the Boston operator thus :

—--- —--- —--- —- -- -- —--- —--- —---
—- -- --

Boston in reply, says : -- -- —---

When Boston calls New York, these signals merely change places.

In acknowledging the receipt of a dispatch, Boston replies with - - —— —---, or sometimes precede the O K with the letter I a few times.

No communication is ever sent until the office to receive it has been called, and a reply has been returned ; and no message is ever regarded as transmitted until the office receiving it gives O K, or commences to send back other dispatches.

Some lines number all their messages which are not D. H., each office commencing in the morning, or whenever its day's business begins (sometimes 6 P.M.), with No. 1 for each message having a destination different from others, then putting No. 2 on the next one going to the same place, and so on ; so that no two messages, sent to the same place, from any *one* place in one day, will have the same number on them. If an office sends 20 messages to one station in one day the numbers will run from 1 up to 20. If dispatches go to 20 offices, one to each, all of them will bear No. 1. The loss of a communication is much less likely to occur when it is thus marked. In transmitting messages thus numbered, the number is the first thing that is sent : "Fr" comes directly after it.

When an operator discovers that he makes a telegraphic character wrong, he corrects himself by re-writing the word in which the error occurs ; and if he sends a wrong word and detects his mistake, he says, "Msk" (mistake), and goes back to the word preceding.

It is the duty of every operator to count the number of words in the body of every message he receives, and if his counting does not agree with the number sent over the line, to immediately inform the sender of the fact, by stating how many words he has received. The operator sending them counts his copy also, and, if he finds that there has been a miscount of the original message, he corrects his check ; but if he sees that the words are correctly counted, he begins to repeat the body of the message, and proceeds until the operator receiving discovers the error.

Sometimes the initials only are repeated. The main object of counting messages in offices receiving them is to avoid incorrect transmission.

If, while receiving anything over a line, an operator for any reason does not get it satisfactorily, he at once calls for a repetition of the unintelligible part by using some abbreviation, meaning "go ahead" or "start at," and writing the last word which he gets perfectly.

The operator receiving a dispatch should always mark on the blank, in a place provided for that purpose, the hour and minute of its reception, and the one sending must put on the face of his copy, in some convenient place, the hour and minute at which he sends it, and sometimes also the initials of both sender and receiver, and the name or number of the wire on which it is sent. Some offices mark, on one corner of original messages, the time at which they are received from the public.

ABBREVIATIONS

are used in conversation, news reports, office, and other D. H. messages, and about *paid* messages, but never in the *body* of them. The number of abbreviations in use on the various lines is quite large, but those which are used alike by all are comparatively few. Numerical abbreviations differ so greatly in their meaning on different lines, that it is deemed best not to lumber the student with information which he may have to unlearn.

The following list, including those which have one signification on all lines, will give the student such a start that he can easily learn others from their connection :

Abv.	Above.	Btn.	Between.
Ads.	Address.	Btr.	Better.
Ae.	Are.	Bsns.	Business.
Af.	After	C.	Can.
Ay.	Any	Cc.	Commence.
Abt.	About.	Cur.	Current.
Agn.	Again.	Col.	Collect.
Ahr.	Another.	Cd.	Could.
Amt.	Amount.	Ci.	Circuit.
Ans.	Answer.	Ck.	Check.
B.	Be.	Cm.	Come.
Bf.	Before.	Co.	Company.
Bk.	Back. Book.	Cmn.	Common.
Bn.	Been.	Com.	Communication.
Bat.	Battery.	Condr.	Conductor.
Bbl.	Barrel.	Chgs.	Charges.
Brk.	Break.	Dd.	Did.

Dg.	Doing.
D. H.	Free.
Dn.	Done.
Ds.	Does.
Dw.	Down.
E.	Of the.
Eh.	Each.
Ehr.	Either.
Ex.	Express.
F.	Of.
Fi.	Fire.
Fr.	From.
Frt.	Freight.
Fwd.	Forward.
Fig.	Figure.
Guar.	Guaranteed.
G. A.	Go Ahead.
Gd	Good.
Gg.	Going.
Gi.	Give.
G. M.	Good Morning.
Gn.	Gone. Good Night.
G.	Ground.
H.	Have.
Ha.	Has.
Hd	Had.
Hf.	Half.
Hm.	Him.
Ho.	Who.
Hr.	Hear. Here.
Hs.	His.
Hu.	House.
Hw.	How.
Hy.	Heavy.
Htl.	Hotel.
Ik.	Like.
Immy.	Immediately.
Inst.	Instrument. Instant.
Impsb.	Impossible.
Impt.	Important.
K.	Take.
Kg.	Taking.
Kn.	Taken.
Kp.	Keep.
Kps.	Compliments.
Kw.	Know.
Lv.	Leave.
Lrn.	Learn.
Ltr.	Letter.
Ltl.	Little.
Ma.	May.
Md.	Made.
Mk.	Make.
Mkg.	Making.
Mh.	Much.
Mr.	More. Mister.
Mt.	Meet.
Mv.	Move.
Min.	Minute.
Msk.	Mistake.
Mtr.	Matter.
Msg.	Message.
Msngs.	Messenger.
Nh.	North.
N.	Not.
Na.	Name.
Ni.	Night.
Nn.	None.
No.	Number.
Nr.	Near.
Ns.	News.
Nvr.	Never.
Nsy.	Necessary.
Ntg.	Nothing.
N. M.	No more.
O. K.	Correct.
Ovr.	Over.
Obg.	Oblige.
Ofs.	Office.
Ohr.	Other.
Op.	Operator.
Pa.	Pay.
Pc.	Place.
Pd.	Paid.
P. O.	Post Office.
Pls.	Please.
Ppr.	Paper.
Psb.	Possible.
Qk.	Quick.
Qt.	Quite.

R.	For.	Tnk.	Thank.
Rr.	Repeat. Railroad.	Tm.	Them. To-morrow.
Rs.	Raise.	Tn.	Then.
Rt.	Right.	Tr.	Their. There.
Rhr.	Rather.	Ts.	This.
Rtn.	Return.	Ty.	They.
S.	Was.	Tel.	Telegraph.
Sa.	Same.	Tho.	Though.
Sd.	Should. Said.	Trn.	Train.
Sh.	Such.	Thot.	Thought.
Sl.	Shall.	Thru.	Through.
Sm.	Some.	U.	You.
Sn.	Soon.	Ur.	Your.
Su.	South.	Ut.	But.
Ss.	Says.	Un.	Under.
St.	Street.	Und.	Understand.
Sfb.	Stop for breakfast.	V.	Very.
Sfd.	" " dinner.	W.	Will.
Sft.	" " tea.	Wa.	Way.
Sfn.	" " the night.	Wd.	Would.
Sig.	Signature.	Wh.	Which.
Sml.	Small.	Wi.	With. Wire.
Stk.	Stock.	Wk.	Week. Weak.
Smtg.	Something.	Wl.	Well.
Stix.	Sticks.	Wn.	When.
T.	The.	Wr.	Where.
Tt.	That.	Ws.	West.
Td.	To-day.	Wt.	What.
Tff.	Tariff.	Wy.	Why.
Tg.	Thing.	Whr.	Whether.
Ti.	Time.	Wrd.	Word.
Tk.	Think.	X.	Next.

Besides the foregoing, there are several large classes of wo having certain terminations, which are abbreviated in a regu manner.

The termination	ing	drops	in.
	ed	"	e.
	ion or ian	"	io or ia.
	ive	"	ie.
	ial	"	ia.
	ble	"	e.
	ful	"	u.
	ess	"	es

PART II.

PRACTICAL SCIENCE.

GENERAL PRINCIPLES OF ELECTRO-MAGNETIC TELEGRAPHS.

All telegraphs effecting communication by means of Magnets, produced by electric currents, are styled *Electro-Magnetic ;* and in each are to be found five principal parts, as follows :

Conductors, for conveying the motive power—*electricity*—between spaces more or less distant.

Insulators, to confine the electric current to the conductor.

Batteries, for producing the motive power.

Magnets, with the appurtenances, to be actuated by electricity.

Manipulating keys, for controlling the current.

CONDUCTORS AND INSULATORS.

To make lightning our obedient servant we must understand that there are certain substances through which it will readily pass, while other bodies allow it to move with great difficulty, or entirely obstruct its passage. The first-named are *conductors*, the others *non-conductors* or *insulators*. In these two general classes are found many shades of difference, so that there are all degrees of conducting power, from the best conductor to the best insulator. Metals and their alloys rank first as good conductors. Among the best of these are silver and copper, different authorities placing different ones at the head, while iron and platinum, as regards their power of conduction, are quite low in this class. The only non-metallic substance whose conductibility at all approaches that of the metals is carbon, well calcined. Other forms of this element, as charcoal and plumbago, conduct in a less degree, while the diamond, which is pure crystallized carbon, is a good insulator. Some acids, saline solutions, moist earth, animals, and green vegetables, are conductors in a still smaller degree. Pure water is yet lower in the scale, and, when frozen so as to be perfectly dry, is a non-conductor.

There is a great variety of substances having so feeble a power of conduction that they are regarded as non-conductors. Among such are chalk, lime, marble, and stone generally ; rust of metals, fibrous substances, as wood, when dry, leather, parchment, feathers, papers, hair, wool, silk and cotton. Dry air, sulphur, rosin, sealing wax, gutta percha, shellac, rubber and glass, are the best of insulators. Any substance reduced to a powder becomes a conductor to a certain extent, on account of its absorption of moisture. Frictional electricity, which is vastly more intense than galvanic, can pass through glass only by making a fracture ; hence, glass may be said to be an absolute non-conductor.

As oxides of metals can scarcely be considered conductors, all joints in a wire, over which an electric current is to pass, should, when formed, be perfectly clean. In making a splice in a wire enough of the two ends to form a joint should first be brightened, and then each wire should be firmly wound around the other (Fig. 1), the different convolutions touching one another, and

***Fig*. 1.**

passing, as near as may be, at right angles with the wire which they surround. A wire, in being spliced, must never be bent back and wound upon itself, forming a loose loop, which, for telegraphic purposes, is very unreliable.

In splicing two wires in an office, each one should be given eight or ten convolutions ; but four or five will answer for the line wire, because the strain on it always keeps those joints firm.

Splices in offices, however, should be avoided as much as possible.

It must be noticed that, in order to keep a current of electricity confined to a wire over which it is wished to pass, the wire must not be permitted to touch other conductors in such a manner that the current will run off on them. This is accomplished by suspending the wire on *insulators* ; and when thus separated from other conducting bodies it is said to be *insulated.* Glass and vulcanized rubber are articles chiefly employed in the insulation of telegraph lines. A section of the glass insulator, and the manner in which it is atached to the pole, are exhibited in Fig. 2. B is a bracket, usually of oak, which is spiked to the pole P. Over the upper part of the bracket fits the glass G. The line wire passes by the side of the glass, to which it is fastened by a "tie" wire. The glass on the under side is concave, for the purpose of keeping that portion dry during wet weather, to prevent the current from passing from the wire to the pole.

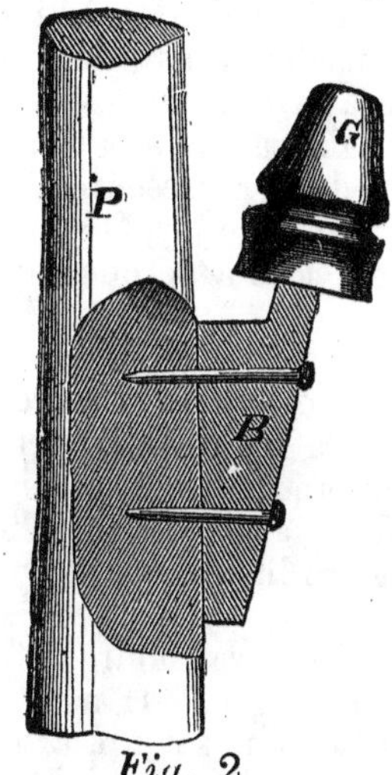

Fig. 2

GALVANIC BATTERIES.

In the fluid of each cup of every galvanic battery two pieces of solid conductor are placed, one end of each projecting above the fluid. These ends are termed *poles.* One of these pieces is always *zinc;* the other, some finer metal, or carbon.

A battery will generate no electricity, except while some unbroken conductor is touching *both* poles, or the poles themselves are in contact with each other. The conductor, as of wire, may be any length, and the battery will force electricity through it if the continuity be perfect, but the slightest imaginable opening in any portion of the wire will completely obstruct the passage of any electricity. The flow of electricity is known under the name of *current :* while *circuit* is the term applied to the conductor, or *path* for the current. The metals and fluids in the battery, as well as the wire, are to be considered a portion of the *circuit.*

An important principle to be continually borne in mind is, *that a current cannot be made to start from one pole of a battery unless it can pass around and touch the other pole, be the distance a few inches or a thousand miles.*

There are but three kinds of batteries in general use on telegraph lines—the Grove, the Carbon and the Daniell, or blue vitriol.* The last is the only one here considered, as it is the one generally, if not universally employed at all stations where young operators are likely to be called on to take care of a battery.

The Daniell battery is usually constructed as represented in Fig. 3, in which G is a glass or glazed earthenware jar, C a cylinder of copper, open at the side and bottom, P C a porous cup, and Z a cylinder or rod of zinc.

A pocket is formed on the outer and upper side of the copper, for the purpose of holding extra crystals of blue vitriol to keep up the strength of the solution. Sometimes an independent pocket, suspended on the glass jar, is used, and the copper is, in some instances, formed into a perfect jar, so that the glass jar is dispensed with ; but such cups are liable to become leaky.

This battery, thus put together, must stand several hours with closed circuit before it will acquire much strength. If a new battery of this kind is required to work as soon as set up, after placing the cups end cylinders in their proper position, the blue vitriol should be pulverized and put into the copper pocket, and then warm water (not hot enough to break the glass) filtered through it until the solution reaches within about two inches of the top of the jar. Then warm or hot water should be poured into the porous cup until the surfaces of the water and the blue vitriol solution are on a level with each other. The addition of six or eight drops of sulphuric acid, half a teaspoonful of white vitriol (sulphate of zinc), or of common salt, to the water in the porous cup, will cause the battery to start off with nearly full force. This battery, as generally constructed and used for local

*Since the above was written, the Hill and Calland Gravity Batteries have come into general use on most Telegraph Lines. In these Batteries the porous cell is dispensed with, the two solutions being separated by their respective specific gravities. EDITOR.

circuits, will run without any attention for ten or fifteen days, according to the length and size of the wire in the local magnet, and the number of office hours per day. If the blue vitriol solution is kept saturated, whenever the battery becomes too much weakened the zincs must be taken out and scraped, and the water in the porous cup, with the exception of a tablespoonful or two of the clear to each cup, must be thrown out and replaced with clean water. If no reservations of the old water (solution of sulphate of zinc) be made, and nothing but pure water be used, the battery, after cleaning, will be very weak for some time. The blue vitriol solution will last a year or more, or until it becomes too filthy from external causes

It is well for every operator to understand that blue vitriol is oxide, or rust of copper, dissolved in sulphuric acid. The action of the battery separates the acid from the copper ; the latter being deposited on the copper cylinder, and the former passing through the porous cup and uniting with the zinc, produces white vitriol, or sulphate of zinc. Therefore, the growth of the copper in thickness, and a corresponding diminution of the zinc, are neither mysterious nor illegitimate.

Once in two or three months the copper should be taken out and the deposit peeled off. This may be done several times, when the deposit will adhere too firmly to the original plate to be removed. Then, when so much copper accumulates as to afford too little room for the porous cup, new coppers must be brought into service.

The porous cups also become coated with copper on the outside, which, after a while, so fills up the pores as to render the cups worthless.

Neglect to keep a surplus of blue vitriol in the pocket designed for that purpose will allow the upper portion of that solution to become weak, and in consequence another current (on the principle of a battery formed of one metal and two fluids) is set up, which eats holes through the copper cylinder where the solution has become exhausted.

The blue vitriol solution, by the combined action of evaporation and absorption, creeps slowly up the sides of the jar, and runs over the top and down the outside. This feature of the Daniell battery may be obviated by rubbing a little oil, melted tallow, or paraffine, on the inside of the jar above the solution, or by occasionally wetting the fingers and pushing down the crystals as they appear at the top of the jar.

In this battery the copper pole is the *positive.* The zinc is the *negative* in this and every other kind of battery now in use.

In joining together any number of cups, whether of the same or of different kinds of battery, the positive pole of the first cup must be connected with the negative of the second, the positive of the second with the negative of the third, and so on throughout the whole series. It matters not which pole we commence with if we are only careful never to connect like poles ; but this law must be as strictly observed in joining batteries hundreds of miles apart as if they stood side by side.

No battery should be permitted to freeze, for while frozen the current is very much impaired, or altogether suspended. A battery, while warm, works more vigorously, as heat is a promoter of chemical action. The connections must be kept free from rust and dirt, in order to allow the current to pass through them freely.

MAGNETS.

A piece of metal that will attract another at a perceptible distance, and with a force greater than that of gravitation, which is a property of all matter, is a *magnet.* The number of substances susceptible of the magnetic property may be limited to five ; nickel, cobalt, iron, and two of its compounds. These compounds—steel (carburet of iron) and loadstone (an iron ore)—form permanent *magnets.* Magnets of *soft iron* are altogether used for telegraphic purposes, on account of their superior magnetic power and the great rapidity with which they acquire and lose it. The softer the iron the quicker its action ; and, therefore, for temporary magnets, it is thoroughly annealed.

If a piece of soft iron be placed near a wire over which a current of electricity is passing, the iron, under the influence of the electric current, will be instantly magnetized, *although the two do not touch each other*, and will attract any other substance that can be similarly affected under the same influence. The moment the flow of electricity stops, the iron ceases to be a magnet ; and thus it can be magnetized and de-magnetized far more rapidly than any hand can vibrate. A bar of iron can not only become magnetic from a current not in contact with it, but can also impart this force to another piece of iron at a perceptible distance : in fact, there can be no attraction until this has taken place, when each attracts the other with the same force ; hence, *magnets attract nothing but magnets, and this attraction is always mutual.* There are other means by which this peculiar property may be given to iron, but none of them have any bearing on telegraphy.

Nearly all the magnetic force of an iron bar accumulates at the ends, which are termed *poles;* and these poles, on account of a strange difference in their action, are distinguished by *north* and *south.* A north pole always *repels* a north, the same as do two souths; but north and south always *attract* each other. One end of *every* magnet has north polarity, and the other end has that of south; hence, one pole of a magnet always attracts the other. To obtain the full power of a magnet it must be bent in the middle, so that the ends come near each other, and then both poles may be brought to act on the same object. When a piece of soft iron is presented to the poles of the magnet the effect of the latter on the former is uniformly such as to set up an attraction between the two; that is, one pole cannot generate the same polarity in another piece of metal so that the two will repel each other. If, instead of bringing a rod of iron near a straight wire carrying an electric current, a long wire be completely covered with silk, or some other non-conductor, and then wound several hundred times round the iron rod, as thread is put on a spool, the magnetic effect of a given current through the wire will be vastly augmented. The object of covering the wire with silk (insulating it) is to keep the different convolutions from touching one another, so as to compel the current to follow the whole length of the conductor.

Let us take a rod of iron eight or ten inches in length, and about half an inch in diameter, and bend it into the form of the letter U; then make of some non-conducting material, as hard rubber, two spools, each about three inches long, and the ends an inch and a quarter in diameter, and fill them with insulated copper wire. Next, slip these spools on the limbs of the bent rod, join the wire of the two spools, and we shall have an electro-magnet, very much like some in use on telegraph lines. Both spools should be wound in the same direction, and, in joining them, both inside or both outside ends of the wires, should be firmly twisted together, after the silk covering has been removed for a short distance and the ends of the wires have been brightened. If one inside should be connected with one outside end, the current through one helix would neutralize the effect of the other helix, so that no magnet would be produced. In such a case a current through either half of the wire would magnetize the iron, but not when passed through both helices.

THE KEY.

For stopping and starting the current on a wire, or, in telegraph phrase, *opening* and *closing circuit,* instead of holding the two ends of a wire in the hands, and striking them together, the key, a device for a more convenient, rapid and uniform movement, is thus arranged: A movable metallic lever, *M*, Fig. 4, on an arbor, is supported by screws in the elevated sides of a metallic base, *B*. Directly beneath *M* is another piece of metal, *A*, which is separated from *B* by some non-conductor (usually vulcanized rubber). On the top and in the centre of *A* is fastened a small piece of platinum wire, and directly above, on the lever *M*, is another piece of the same metal. A screw enters the base at *D*, and serves to fasten the key firmly to the table, and, at the same time, hold one end of the wire to be operated. In the same manner another one screws into *A*, to help to bind the key to the table, and hold the other end of the wire. Now, as *A* is insulated from *B*, the current cannot pass from one to the other, except while *M* is pressed down, bringing together the two platinum points, which are, in reality, the two ends of the wire. As a light spring, under *M*, is nearly always employed, keeping the platinum points separated, whenever the hand leaves the key, a *circuit closer*, *C*, is added. This is a movable brass arm screwed to the base, so that it can slide under a lip on *A*, thus keeping *A* and *B* electrically connected while the key is not in use. When either *M* or *C* touches *A*, the key and circuit are said to be *closed*. *Both* must be away from *A* in order to *open* or *break* crcuit. The back end of *M* is furnished with a screw to regulate the amount of movement which the lever is desired to have. The finger piece of both lever and circuit closer is some non-conductor, to protect the operator from receiving an electric shock from the wire to which the key is attached.

MORSE SYSTEM OF TELEGRAPHY.

The Morse system of communication does not consist in the manner in which the line is built, nor in the kind of battery used on it, as all systems are alike in these respects; but it depends on the method of applying the current to the magnets, the appurtenances of the magnets, and the peculiar mode of causing one current to operate others.

If a magnet, such as last described, be placed in New York, and one end of the wire connected with the earth by means of some good conductor, and from the other end of the magnet wire another one of sufficient length be extended to Washington—care being taken to have it touch nothing but insulators between the two cities—and this long wire attached to one pole of a powerful galvanic battery, the other pole of which is connected with the ground by a third wire, the iron of the magnet in New York will be very sensibly affected by the battery in Washington. If we now take a piece of iron long enough to cover the poles of the magnet, and bring it near them, we will find it to be drawn toward the magnet with a very appreciable force.

We will produce an instrument like a portion of the Morse, by fastening the magnet *M*, Fig. 5, to a dry and finished piece of board, *B*, joining the second piece of iron, *A*, to a small brass bar, and supporting this bar on pivots, also fastened to the wooden base in such a position as to bring the iron near the poles of the magnet. This iron, and the brass bar to which it is attached, must be free to move toward and from the poles of the magnet. This movable portion is known as the *armature*. The distance through which the armature moves is regulated by two brass posts running up from the base, one of them checking the motion toward the magnet, and the other limiting the reverse movement; or two adjustable screws, supported by *one* post, are most frequently employed, in which case it is necessary that the point of the screw checking the backward movement be made of some insulating body. As represented in the figure, every place to which a wire is to be attached is furnished with a binding screw. By attaching to the armature a light spiral spring, pulling in a direction from the magnet, this portion of the instrument is made ready to note electric pulsations. The attractive power of the magnet must, however, overcome the force of the spring.

Now let the wire in Washington be broken, and the magnet in New York will instantly lose its magnetic properties, and, in consequence, the spiral spring will pull the armature back. On joining the wire again in Washington the magnet is simultaneously charged, drawing the armature forward. If the opening and closing the wire be done after the manner of telegraphic characters, the armature in New York will, at the same instant, click out the same letters, so that a sound operator will understand them with the greatest ease.

Such a line may be cut in Philadelphia, and the two ends

thus made be joined to another apparatus, precisely as in New York, when both instruments will be alike operated, and at the same moment. In like manner, and with like results, other instruments may be placed in Baltimore and Washington, and at as many intermediate points as may be desired. The wire may be opened and closed at any other station as well as at Washington. The simultaneous working of all the magnets connected with the line will be effected by breaking and re-establishing the continuity of the wire at *any* point on the route ; and this is, as has already been anticipated, done by means of the key.

By reference to the remarks on batteries it will be understood why the ends of the line were connected with the ground at New York and Washington. The battery was located at the latter place, and, as no current could go to New York without returning to the same battery, we either had to put up a second wire for this purpose, or allow the current to return through the earth, which proves to be better than a return wire, saying nothing of the difference in expense.

Although a battery at Washington will work a line from that place to the metropolis, a second battery at the latter city will improve the working—and a third, placed at Philadelphia, might sometimes be an advantage. Every office, however, must have a key to send messages with, and a magnet with which to receive them.

Again : tracing out a line from New York to Washington, having four offices on it, one in each of these two cities, and also in Philadelphia and Baltimore, commencing at the earth in the first named city, we find a wire running from the earth up into the office, and connecting with one pole of a galvanic battery ; then from the other pole of the battery another wire, running into one of the binding screws of the key ; a third wire then extending from the other binding screw of the key to one end of the wire to the magnet; and from the other end of the magnet wire a fourth wire, running out of the building at the top of the window, and passing along the route,—supported all the way on insulators fastened to poles, to keep the current from passing down to the ground—until the wire reaches Philadelphia, where it enters that office, runs through the magnet and key precisely as in New York, and again emerges from the window. The passage of the line through Baltimore and Washington is nothing but a repetition of what has taken place in the first two cities. In the last named city, the line, after joining the key, magnet, and battery, connects with the earth, the earth joining both ends and completing the circuit.

As any *one* break anywhere in the circuit completely checks all the current throughout the whole line, it follows that all keys must be shut except the one sending a message ; therefore, *two dispatches cannot be sent over one wire at the same time.*

All wire used within offices is of copper. Iron is used for the line wire, on account of its superior strength and greater cheapness.

It is not at all necessary to connect the different parts of the apparatus in the order just described. In passing a line through an office in which are a battery, key, and magnet, it matters not in the least which of them is the first, second, or third to be connected—the only requisite being that they may be joined one after another—for, place the key where you will in the circuit, it will do its labor of starting and stopping the entire current ; the magnet, situated at any point on the line, will be operated, and the battery will send its current over the whole line, if only properly connected at any place. Neither does it make any difference which way the current passes through the key or magnet. The reversal of the current through the magnet reverses the poles, but the polarity of the armature is likewise reversed, so that the working of the magnet remains unchanged.

All such questions as, "Does a message have to be forwarded at every office it is to pass ?" "Which way does a dispatch go over a line ?" and "What is the method of sending in different directions ?" should be satisfactorily answered by the fact that, when a line is in a normal condition, *every* key in the same circuit *always* operates *every* machine situated in it, at the *same instant* and in the *same manner.**

* It is not known whether electricity is a material substance, or merely a property of matter ; and any opinion as to whether its transmission be in the form of a current, by vibrations or otherwise, is sheer speculation. It is simply known that an effect travels with inconceivable rapidity, and seemingly in both directions.

Professor Faraday, in speaking on the nature of electricity before the British Association for the Advancement of Science, thus expressed his views : "There was a time when I thought I knew something about the matter, but the longer I live, and the more carefully I study the subject, the more convinced I am of my total ignorance of the nature of electricity."

When as great an electrician and profound a philosopher as the world has produced arrives at such a conclusion, the student must regard all terms seeming to indicate any form or motion of electricity as nothing more than convenient expressions.

MAIN AND LOCAL CIRCUITS.

A line of telegraph, as thus far represented, is not a very efficient one—and it is not the Morse system *complete*. Although powerful batteries be used on such a line, the great resistance offered by so many miles of wire reduces the strength of the current to such an extent that but a weak magnet can be produced. The motion communicated to the armature of the magnet is too feeble to properly mark paper, or to give as satisfactory a sound as can be obtained by the addition of other batteries and machines in a certain manner.

The armature of the magnet having a motion precisely like that of the key, is converted into one, and used to operate another magnet, Fig. 6, supplied with a current from another battery, Fig. 3. To accomplish this, a battery, Fig. 3, is stationed in the office, usually quite near the instrument, and from one pole of it a wire, *n*, is run to the bottom of the armature of the magnet already described, Fig. 5 ; and from the brass post, which checks the armature in its motion toward the magnet, a second wire, *o*, is connected with another magnet, Fig. 6, and this magnet is, with a third wire, *d*, joined to the other pole of the battery from which the first wire was started. Thus a new and very short circuit is formed of the extra battery, the extra magnet, and the armature of the first magnet. This short, side, or independent circuit, represented by dotted lines, is wholly confined to the office, and is called the *local circuit*. Fig. 6 is a *sounder*, or, in case a *register* is used, it simply takes the place of the sounder, and is connected in the same manner. *Main circuit* is the name given to the one shown in the black lines. The main circuit is the line itself, of which the earth forms one-half. The batteries have the same name as the circuits to which they are attached. The map exhibits no main battery, and does not represent the different parts located *precisely* as they are to be found in an office, but it shows their exact relations, or how they are connected. The local battery is generally placed under the table on which the instruments rest, and only enough of the ends of the wire for connecting the different parts are allowed to come up through the table.*

* For the benefit of such as may desire to construct private Telegraph Lines for business or amusement, the following paragraphs from *Pope's Modern Practice of the Electric Telegraph* are given.

"Arrangement of a Terminal Station.—Fig. 17 is a diagram showing the arrangement of wires, batteries, and instruments for one of the terminal stations of a line.

It must be distinctly understood that the main and the local currents *never* touch each other, and that the *local* exerts no in-

The line wire L, first enters the lightning arrester X, and passes thence through the coils of the relay M, by the binding screws, 1, 2, and thence to the key K, main battery E, and finally to the

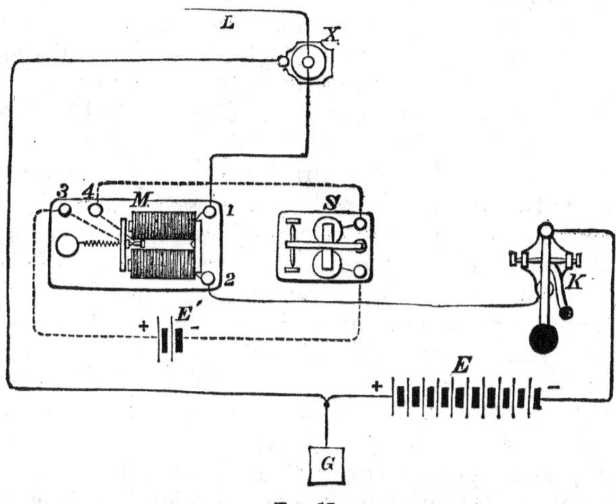

FIG. 17.

ground at G. The local circuit commences at the × pole of the local battery E', and through the platinum points of the relay by the binding screws, 3, 4, thence through the register or sounder coils, S, and back to the other pole of the battery.

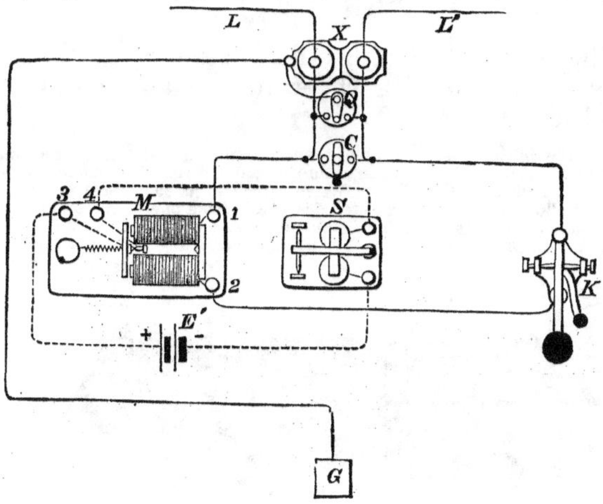

FIG. 18.

ARRANGEMENT OF A WAY STATION.—FIG. 18 shows a plan of the Instruments and connections at a way station.

The line enters at L, passes through the lightning arrester, X, and thence through the relay M,

fluence whatever on the *main*. The only substances which are in contact with the two circuits are the air and the wooden base, *B*, Fig. 5, and both of these are *non-conductors*. The armature, *A*, Fig. 5, closes the local circuit by striking the screw above the magnet. That these two points may be kept bright and make a good connection, they are made of platinum, the same as those of the key; but the tip of the other screw is of some non-conductor, so that the current cannot pass over it when the armature is drawn back by the spring. This armature is simply the key that operates the local circuit, and it may be moved back and forth by the finger, without in the least affecting the line.

Fig. 5 represents the portion of the Morse apparatus known as the *receiving magnet*, because it is the first thing affected by the electric pulsations on the line. *Relay* is the name by which it is known among operators generally. By the map it is seen that every key and relay magnet is situated in the main circuit, and that every relay armature has a local battery and a sounder or register attached to it. The key operates the relay magnet; the relay magnet operates the armature (by attracting without touching it); and the armature works the sounder or register in the same manner that the key affects the relay. The movement of the armature is feeble, but powerful enough to open and close the local, which, on account of the little resistance in so few feet of wire, operates the sounder with many times the force of the armature.

The binding screws fastening the wires *o n* to the relay are permanently connected with the armature and posts by wires beneath its base.

key K, and back to the lightning arrester, and thence to the next station by the line L'. The arrangement of the local circuit is the same as in the last figure. The button C, arranged as shown in the figure, is called a "*Cut Out.*" When turned so as to connect the two wires leading into the office, it allows the line current to pass across from one to the other without going through the instruments. The instruments should always be cut out, by means of this apparatus, when leaving the office temporarily or for the night, and also during a thunder-storm, to

FIG. 21.

avoid damage to the apparatus. FIG. 21 shows a better arrangement. The ground switch Q is used to connect the line with the earth on either side of the instruments at pleasure. It is only used in case of accidents or interruptions on the lines."

On *very short* lines, where it is desired to use sounders *without* relays, the sounders will occupy the position of the relays, and the local circuits will be omitted.—EDITOR.

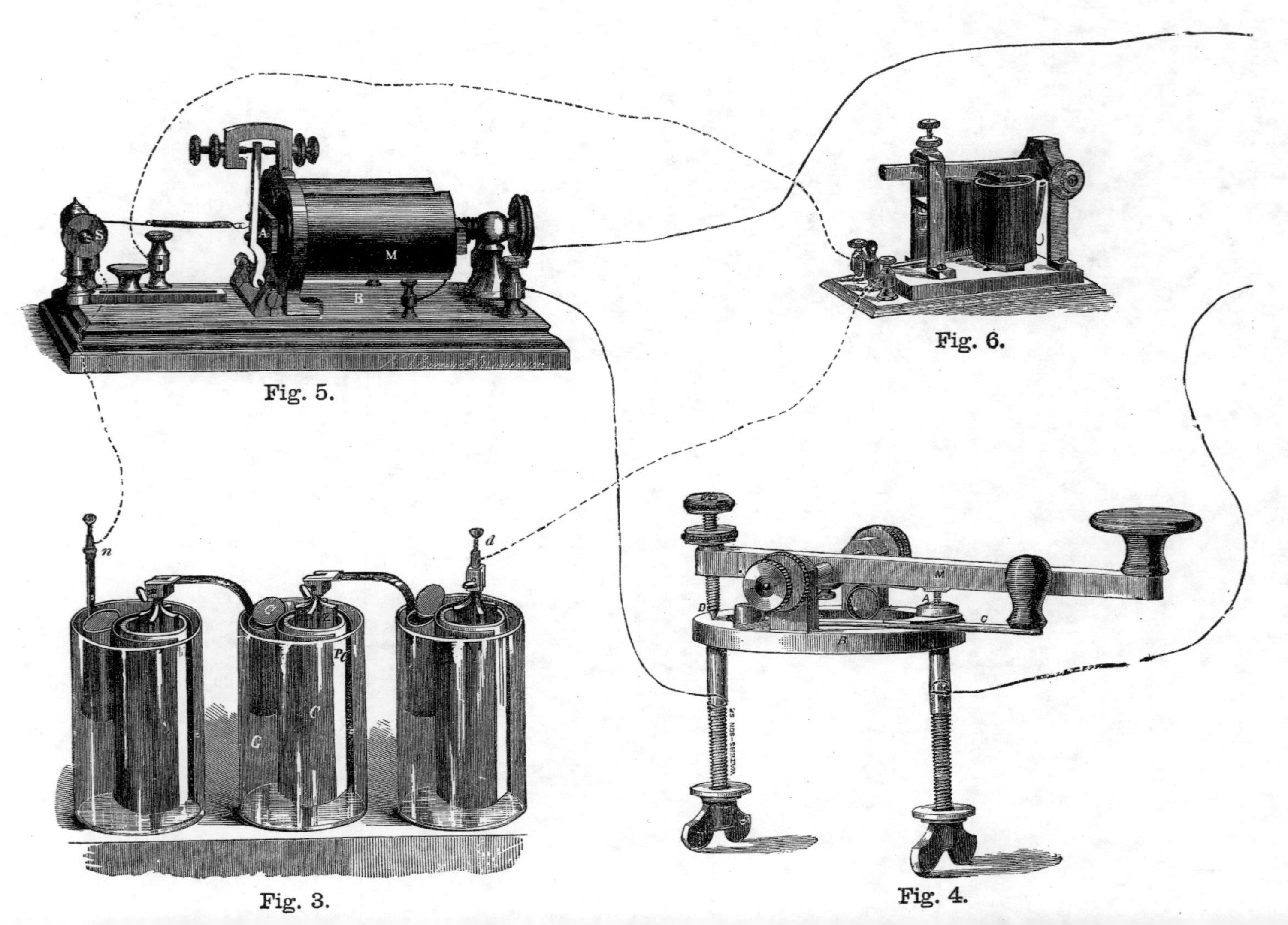

Fig. 5.

Fig. 6.

Fig. 3.

Fig. 4.

TILLOTSON RELAY, No. 1.

MANAGEMENT OF INSTRUMENTS, WIRES, AND BATTERIES.

GROUND WIRES.

If to a line from New York to Washington, having a main battery at the latter place only, some conducting substance be joined, and then connected with the earth as at Philadelphia, the current will pass over this conductor and return to Washington, and no electricity will reach New York to operate that instrument. All machines between the conductor in question and Washington will be worked. Such a wire is named the *ground wire,* and every intermediate office is supplied with one to be used only in case of trouble on the line. When gas or water pipes enter an office, the ground wire is attached to them. Stations not having this excellent means of ground connection fasten a wire to a plate or rod of metal, and bury the piece of metal so that it is always in contact with moist earth.*

If Philadelphia puts his ground wire in contact with the line south of his instrument, and there is a main battery at each end of the line, the currents from both batteries will go only to this ground wire, and passing over it, to or from the earth, as the

*A ground plate should have an area of at least three square feet, and be buried in a perpendicular position. EDITOR.

case may be, will return again to their respective batteries. During this state of things—the current from New York reaching the Philadelphia Machine—these two offices can communicate with each other. The current from Washington not quite reaching the instrument at Philadelphia, does not permit the latter city to hold communication with any office south of it; but Baltimore and Washington can work together at the same time that New York and Philadelphia do. The ground wire divides the line into two independent circuits, and forms a common conductor for both currents, on the same principle that the earth forms one-half of every main circuit.

BREAKS.

Let the line so break between Philadelphia and Baltimore that the ends fall on the ground, and two entirely distinct lines will be the result, and offices on the same side of the break will work with each other as if nothing had happened. Should the southern end of a break be so near a pole as to hang in the air, the circuit south of it would be left open, and Baltimore, in order to work with Washington, would have to complete the circuit with his ground wire. Should he apply it south of his instrument, the current (from Washington) would pass over the ground wire before quite reaching his machine, and his inability to work would show trouble on the line north of him.

The northern end of the break being on the earth, Philadelphia does not use his ground wire to effect communication with New York, but his inability to raise either office south of him, after repeated efforts, leads him to suspect some difficulty on the line. Then, by applying his ground wire north of his instrument, he finds there is no current from the Washington battery. This simply shows him that the line is in some way connected with the earth between him and Washington, probably north of Baltimore, because he cannot be raised; but it by no means proves that the wire is broken.

Should the circuit get open between the two points in an office where the ground wire is applied, no current could be made to pass through that instrument by the use of the ground wire: therefore, whenever an operator cannot get a current from either direction, he should carefully search this portion of the main circuit in his office for an opening in it.

ESCAPES

In picturing a line and its workings, thus far, it has been the supposition that when *any* of the current on a line is broken, *all* of it is, and that the entire current always goes the whole length of the line. This is what is desired, but circumstances frequently render it impossible. Returning again to the same line, and placing a wet rope or a stick of green wood so as to touch both the line and the earth at Philadelphia, we find that only a *portion* of the current passes through the rope or wood, while the *remainder* of it follows the entire length of the line.

Now let New York open his key, and he will take from the line all the current from his own battery, and that portion of the Washington current which does not pass over the poor conductor touching the line at Philadelphia: in other words, he will interrupt just what reaches his key. That from the south, finding its way through the green wood, is still passing over the line from Philadelphia to Washington, and partially magnetizing the relays on this portion of the route, and keeping the local circuits closed when they are wanted to be open, unless the relay spring has sufficient tension to overcome the residual attraction. This leakage of the current from the line to the ground passes under the name of *escape*. Offices on the same side of an escape can communicate with each other as usual, but it is difficult, and sometimes impossible, for an office on one side receiving writing from another station beyond the partial ground wire. Some lines are much annoyed in this manner by the interference of trees, and all lines are affected by rainy or foggy weather. In wet weather every pole and insulator becomes a feeble conductor —and, perhaps, the air itself—thus offering so many inducements for the current to run down to the earth that sometimes it cannot be made to go over fifty miles from the battery, and, of course, a dispatch can be sent no greater distance.

If Washington, testing an escape to determine its location, has Baltimore open his key, and then he (Washington) tries to operate his own instrument but cannot do so—because there is no current left on that end of the line—he knows the escape to be north of Baltimore. Now, if Baltimore closes his key, and the one in Philadelphia is open, and Washington finds that he can work his own machine, or, perhaps communicate with Baltimore, it proves an escape to exist between Baltimore and Philadelphia. Again: if Washington finds a little current left on the line while Baltimore is open, and a still stronger one while Philadelphia has his key open, it shows an escape in two places. To clearly understand the ill effects of escapes, it must be borne in mind that *sending* is a systematic putting on and taking off the current, the cessation being equally as important as the continuance of it. Anything preventing a current from passing on the line is no more injurious than that which will not allow it to be interrupted. The portion of the current which can be broken is all that any use is made of; all the escape is not only of no utility, but it is a real hindrance to an advantageous employment of that remaining on the line.

It sometimes happens that the operating table becomes wet, or is made of wood only partly seasoned, so that a portion of the main current finds a passage through the moisture of the table while the key on it is open. This does not conduct any of the current to the earth, and cannot, therefore, be properly called an escape, though *every* relay in circuit with a key on a moist table must have a high adjustment to receive the writing from such a key. This trouble, however, does not in the least interfere with such office in receiving from other stations, nor does it at all affect other offices in working with one another.

CROSSES.

Another annoyance, of very frequent occurrence on some lines having two or more wires on the same poles, are "crosses," or contact of the different line wires with each other—which, so far as their utility is concerned, reduces to *one* wire all the wires thus joined. Each wire crossed acts as a long ground wire to the others in contact with it. Suppose two wires, designated by Nos. 1 and 2, running on the same pole from New York to Washington, to be twisted together between Philadelphia and Baltimore. Next, suppose No. 1 to be left open in New York, and No 2 in Washington; now, commencing at New York on No. 2, which is closed, and tracing southward over this wire until the cross is reached, and from that point over No. 1 to the southern terminus, we find a complete circuit, though both wires are open; consequently, Washington and Baltimore, on No. 1, can work with Philadelphia and New York on No. 2. If Washington keeps both wires closed, New York or Philadelphia can operate both wires south of the cross by leaving either wire open and writing on the other, because the one wire north of the cross becomes the common conductor for both south of it. This is one mode for detecting and locating a cross. Another method is for New York to ask Philadelphia to try him on No. 2 with No. 1 open, while New York, doing just the reverse, tries Philadelphia on No. 1 with No. 2 open ; and, if they can work with each other on different wires, it shows those wires to be crossed between them. If they cannot get each other, New York tries the same thing with Baltimore, and so on until he gets to an office with which he can work on a different wire. This test determines the cross to be between such office and the first one from that station toward New York. When several wires become tangled, and at different places on the line, the task of locating becomes much more lengthy and difficult, on account of first getting the different offices to test with.

If, instead of opening one wire, New York or Philadelphia should try to work one of them with the other closed, he would operate only that one wire north of the cross, for the other wire north and to the south of it would still form a perfect circuit. The same principle holds true for any number of wires so joined —all but one being useless so long as they remain together, or at least between the two offices nearest the cross, and between which the cross is situated. In case of a cross of two wires between Philadelphia and Baltimore, it is necessary to leave one of them open only between these two cities. The offices may open No. 2, so that New York and Washington may communicate over No. 1 ; then, Philadelphia may put his ground wire on No. 2, leaving it open south of the ground, and work with New York, while Baltimore, in a similar manner, communicates with Washington.

REVERSED CURRENTS.

If on a line from New York to Washington two main batteries be placed, with both positive or both negative poles connected with the earth, no current will pass over the line, though the circuit is complete—for each battery will oppose the other, stopping all galvanic action. With the batteries thus located, let Philadelphia or Baltimore put his ground wire on in either direction, and he will get a current, for the ground wire divides the line into two distinct circuits, each of which will operate without interfering with the other. This is the only case in which there can be a current *each* way with a ground wire on, and *no* current with it off.

An intermediate station, wishing to connect a main battery to the line, first finds out, from some office already having one, the direction of the poles of his battery; but the same thing may be determined in other ways.

When the current from a powerful battery is passed through the arm of an individual, a greater shock is experienced in the arm connected directly with the zinc or negative pole than in the other.

If a circuit be opened, and both ends of the break dipped into water, decomposition of the water will ensue, and the greatest volume of gas will rise from the wire leading directly to the negative pole. Therefore, the positive pole of another battery, required to be put in circuit, must be connected to the wire giving the greatest shock, or evolving the most gas.

ADJUSTMENT AND CARE OF INSTRUMENTS.

The distance through which the armature of the relay should move is very small—say equal to once the thickness of good writing paper. Magnets always retain more or less attraction, even when the circuit is perfectly broken, so that the spring on the armature must always have some tension, and a great deal more during a humid atmosphere than while the air is clear and dry. This tempering of the relay spring according to the amount of magnetism, while a key is open, is *adjusting*; and it is *high* or *low*, as the force of spring is great or small. *This duty is the most important one connected with the management of instruments.* It not only needs to be done several times a day, under the most favorable circumstances, but, from a few times daily, the frequency increases, until the operator must keep hold of the screw *S*, Fig. 5, regulating the spring—turning first one way and then the other nearly all the time he is either sending or receiving. Sometimes the slightest variation from a certain point, in either direction, will cause the instrument to cease working. Under such circumstances adjusting is very difficult, but in a large majority of instances it requires only the memory and the will to do it. The tempering of the relay spring is also perplexing, as well as the location of the trouble difficult, when a cross or an escape is a "swinging" one; that is, when a wire keeps swinging against another or against a tree, but remaining in contact only a short time.

Thunder storms vary the current over a line so suddenly and to such a degree as to cause the most difficult adjustment, at times rendering transmission utterly impossible, besides endangering the wire of the relay magnet, which is sometimes burned with a flash, accompanied by a sharp report.

The Aurora Borealis sometimes influences the wire in a similar manner, but less violently, never causing any harm other than a suspension of business. Several forms of *lightning arresters* have been made and used for conducting atmospheric electricity from the line to the earth. It matters but little whether it is led to the ground or not, if it is only diverted from the relay magnet. Every operator can make one of two pieces of wire and a vial of water. A short piece of wire (six inches long), considerably larger than that in the relay magnet, run from each main circuit binding screw of the relay, and the ends dipped into a small bottle of water, forms one of the best protections against lightning. The distance of the wires from each other in the water, as also their depth in it, may be varied, but they must not be allowed to come together. Water being a poor conductor of galvanic electricity, only a small portion of the current will pass through it, the larger part choosing the magnetic wire; but atmospheric electricity, being possessed of enormous intensity, prefers the short water route. None of these devices, however, are an absolute safeguard; but during a severe thunder storm relays should be disconnected from the line, and in such a manner as to leave no break in the main circuit.

The local circuit, being confined to the office, is subject to none of the fluctuations of the main. The local battery simply grows weak by use, when it has to be renewed. The spring on the arm of the local (sounder or register) magnet merely requires weakening as the battery working it becomes exhausted. The iron part of this arm must never come so near the poles of the magnet that one thickness of ordinary writing paper will not pass between them. If permitted to touch, the magnet discharges slowly. The same truth applies to the relay magnet and its armature.

The platinum points of the key, and more frequently those of the armature of the relay, burned and roughened by the current, sometimes fail to break circuit. The remedy is to rub them gently with a very fine file, or draw between them a strip of clean paper.

If a relay "sticks" (fails to break circuit,) it troubles only the office where that relay is located. If a key "sticks," it interferes with both sender and receiver.

MORSE CHARACTERS.

A	- —	O	- -	1	- — — -	Period	- - — — - -
B	— - - -	P	- - - - -	2	- - — - -	Comma	- — - —
C	- - -	Q	- - — -	3	- - - — -	Semicolon	- — - — -
D	— - -	R	- - -	4	- - - - —	Interrogation	— - - — -
E	-	S	- - -	5	— — —	Exclamation	— — — -
F	- — -	T	—	6	- - - - - -	Parenthesis	- — - - —
G	— — -	U	- - —	7	— — - -	Italics	— - - - —
H	- - - -	V	- - - —	8	— - - - -	Paragraph	— — — —
I	- -	W	- — —	9	— - - —		
J	— - — -	X	- — - -	0	——		
K	— - —	Y	- - - -				
L	——	Z	- - - -				
M	— —	&	- - - -				
N	— -						

L. G. TILLOTSON & CO.,

5 & 7 DEY ST., NEW YORK.

PRICE LIST

OF

Telegraph Machinery

AND SUPPLIES.

CABLES, OFFICE & MAGNET WIRES,

(Fourteenth Edition.)

FACTORY, 139, 141 and 143 CENTRE STREET.

REGISTER SET, COMPLETE—CUBAN STYLE.

$75.00 Per Set, Complete.

Our Combination Morse Instruments received the *First Premium* over all competitors at the Cincinnati Industrial Exhibition.

L. G. Tillotson & Co.'s Price List.

[*To Purchasers:* Orders by mail and telegraph for any Instruments, Batteries, or material herein described, in large or small quantities, will have as prompt attention as though ordered in person. Give your address in full, including County and State. To prevent loss, Remittances should be sent by Postal Money-Order, Draft, Registered Letter, or by Express. Orders for goods to be sent C. O. D. to points far distant from New York, should be accompanied by remittance amounting to one-third of the bill ordered.]

INSTRUMENTS.

REGISTERS.

L. G. T. & Co.'s Improved European Register, with extra long Spring and perfect Governor. The works of this Register are completely protected from dust by plate-glass covers, and it is the most perfect Morse Register ever made.

Price $65 00

[Our Register, received the first premium over all competitors at the Cincinnati Industrial Exposition.]

INSTRUMENTS.

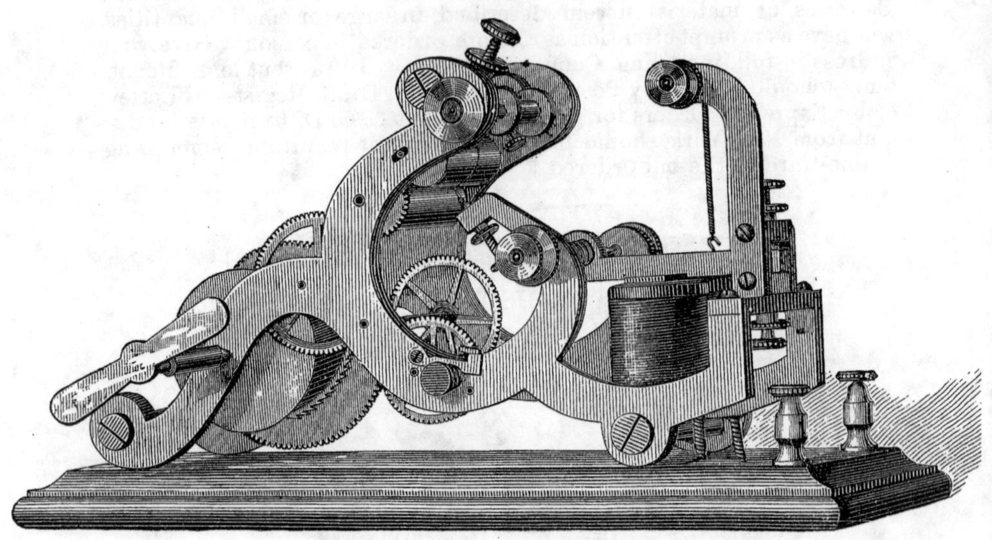

L. G. T. & CO.'S PREMIUM REGISTER No. 1.

With weight or spring. A perfect sounder with the paper in or out.

Register No. 1, Spring, Premium Pattern	$47 50
" " 1, Weight, " "	45 00
" " 2, "	38 00
" Cords, Cat-Gut	0 35
" " Brass, per foot	0 05
" Winding Keys	1 25
" Weights with Pulleys	2 25
" " without Pulleys	1 75
" Paper, per pound	0 24
" " " " by the case	0 21
" Reels, (Adjustable)	3 00
" " Finished Brass	6 50

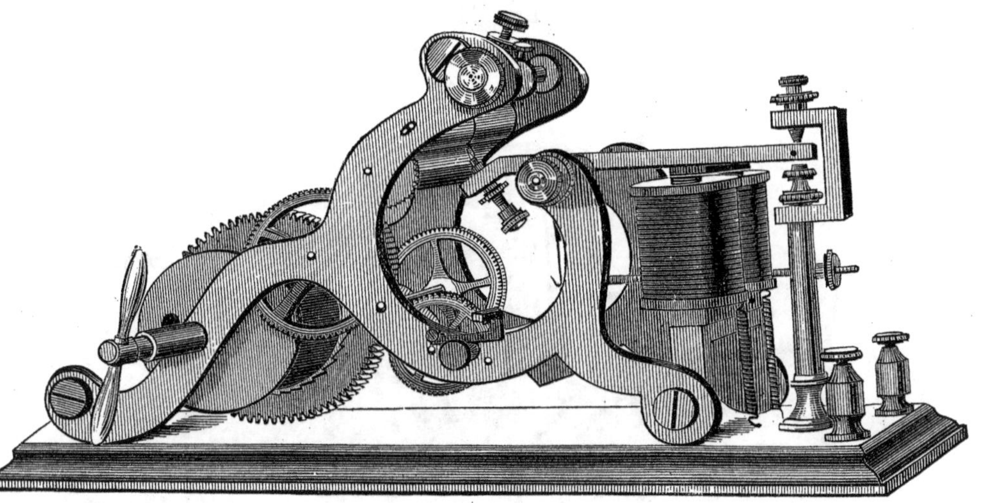

No. 2 REGISTER, $38.00.

RELAYS.

Our No. 1 Relays are finely finished and mounted on polished Rosewood Bases, with polished rubber-covered magnets, wound with our patent glazed or with best fine silk-covered pure copper wire, having soldered connections and firm nut fastenings throughout, and the latest improved extension adjustments. They are accurately measured, and the Resistance stamped on the Base.

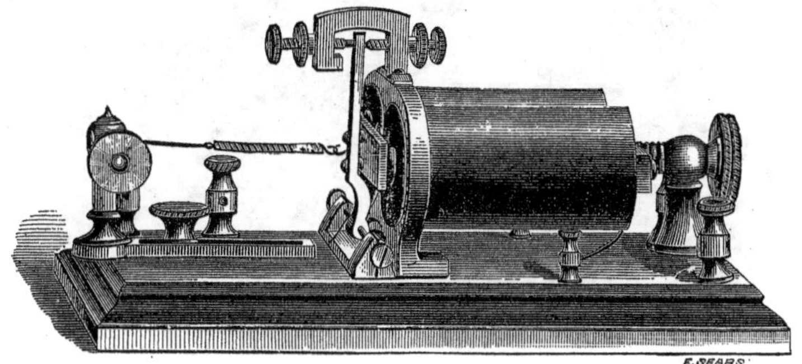

No. 1, Low Resistance, 50 to 100 ohms.................... $15 00
" 1, Standard Size, Resistance, 110 to 160 ohms........... 16 00

INSTRUMENTS.

Relays.

No. 1, Extra Heavy Magnets, Resistance, 160 to 600 ohms $18.00

No. 2, 50 to 400 ohms. 12.00

No. 2, Light resistance, 20 to 100 ohms 10.00

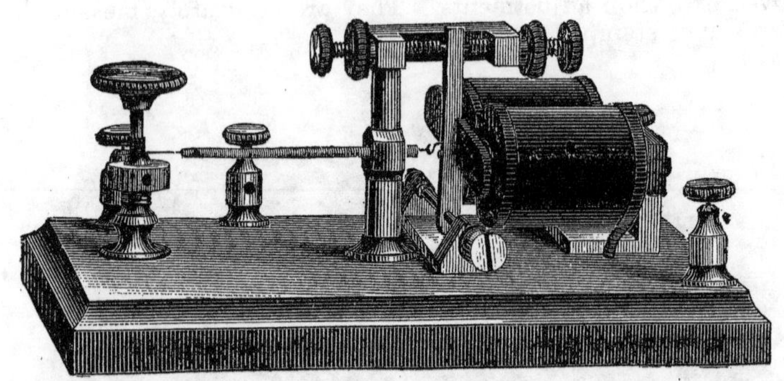

Pony, 20 to 50 ohms, for lines 5 to 30 miles, ... $7.50

Pony, 60 to 100 ohms, ... 8.50

INSTRUMENTS.

Relays.

No. 1, Box Sounding, Tillotson, any required resistance.......$16 00
" 2, " " " " " " 14 00

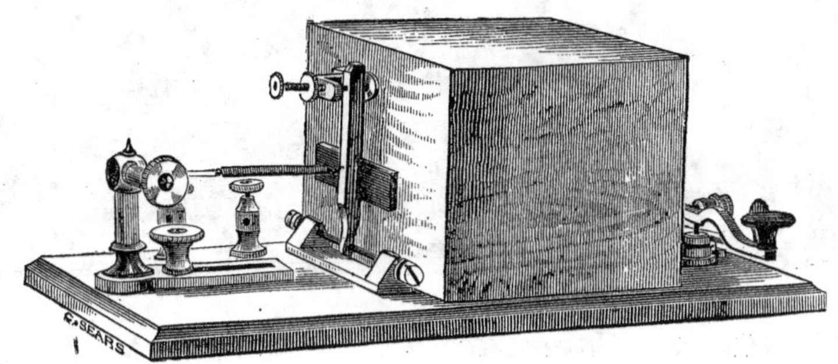

[Our Improved Box, Relays are excellent wrecking instruments.]

No. 1, Box Sounding, Tillotson, No. 1, Key on Base..........$23 50
" 1, " " " No. 2, Key on Base...... ... 22 50
" 3, " " " No. 3, Key on Base.... .. . 20 00

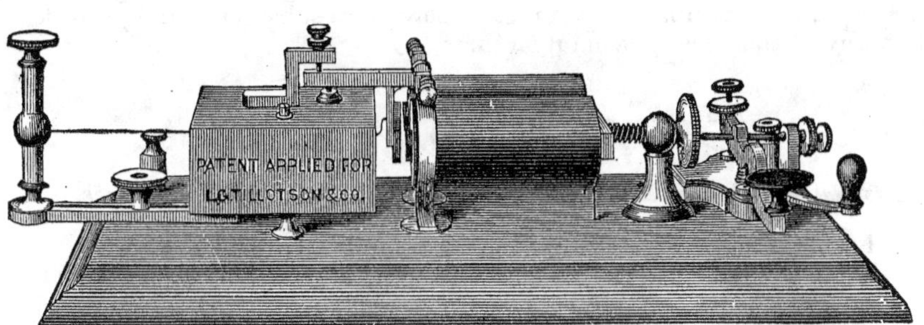

Tillotson's Patent Combination Key on Base No. 1.... ....$30 00
" " " " " " No. 2 .... 26 00
Relay Springs, per doz 60

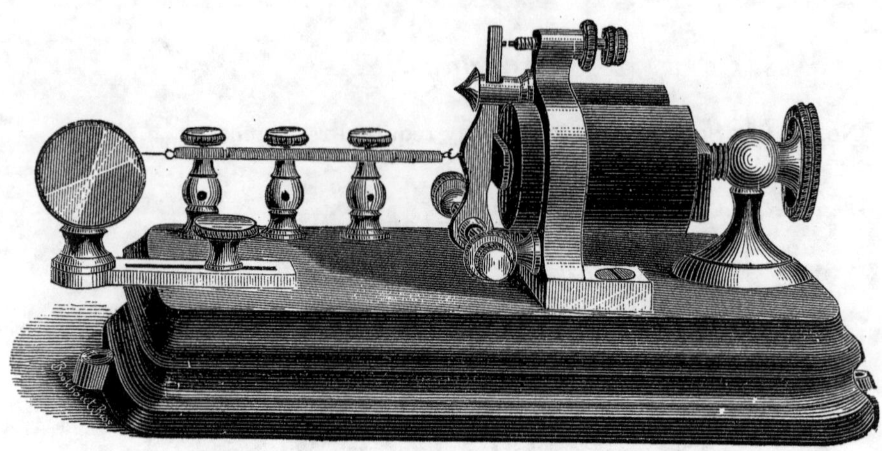

Western Union Relay. Price, $16.00.

With all latest improvements in adjustments, bearings and connections. Magnets wound with *very best silk-covered pure copper wire*, tested to highest standard of conductivity.

The chief objection to this style of Relay, as it is generally made, is found in the rubber studs through which trunnion screws of armature lever pass, and the rubber post through which top adjusting screws pass; as these rubber pieces are easily and frequently broken off. Our substitution for these of solid metal posts dispenses entirely with this objection, making the complete Relay more substantial and perfect than any of this class yet manufactured.

COMBINATION SETS.

Finely finished: Mounted upon Polished Rosewood Bases.

No. 1, Light Resistance Relay, 50 to 100 ohms, No, 5 Key and No. 2 Sounder....................................$26 00

No. 1, Standard Relay, 150 ohms, No. 1, Giant, Railroad, or Pony Sounder and No. 3 Key.......................... 29 50

No. 1, High Resistance Relay, No. 1, Giant, Railroad, or Pony Sounder and No. 2 Key.......................... 32 00

Complete Combined Set of Instruments for one Office, No. 1 or Western Union Relay, Giant Sounder, Caton Key, Lightning Arrester, Ground Switch and Cut-out.............. 35 00

The Perfection of Main-Line Sounding Relays.

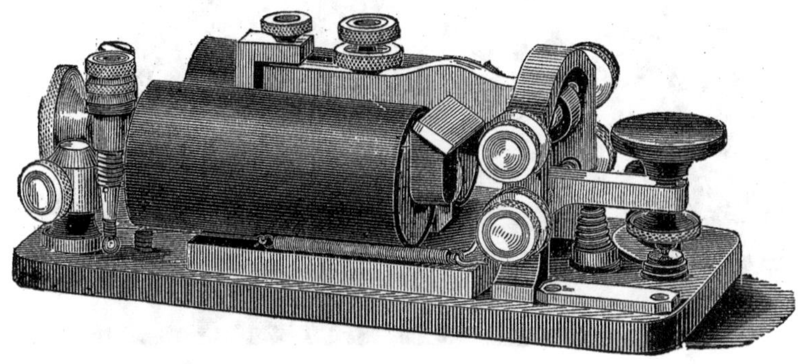

The Little Giant Pocket Relay.

In the form of Pocket Relays, as shown above, or for use on Main Line in offices without Locals, these splendid Instruments are, in all practical respects, and in EXTERNAL BEAUTY, as near ABSOLUTE PERFECTION as can be desired.

As this form is so entirely new, and so far superior to any others hitherto made, it should be seen by all Superintendents, and tried on every Railway Telegraph Line, with a view to its adoption as the Standard Instrument for Wrecking Sets and Office purposes.

Size of Case, $2\frac{1}{2}$x$2\frac{3}{4}$x$5\frac{3}{4}$.

SOUNDING QUALITIES EQUAL TO THOSE OF THE LARGEST AND BEST BOX RELAYS.

Price, in fine finished case........................$22 00

POCKET INSTRUMENTS.

No. 1. Fine Finish, Hard Rubber Case, $1\frac{1}{4}$x$2\frac{1}{2}$x5 inches. $18.00

No. 1. Nickel Plated, " " " " 20.00

No. 2. Fine Finish, Hard Rubber Case, $1\frac{1}{4}$x$2\frac{1}{2}$x5 inches. $16.00

No. 2. Nickel Plated, " " " " 18.00

[Our Pocket Relays received the first premium over all competitors at the Cincinnati Industrial Exposition.]

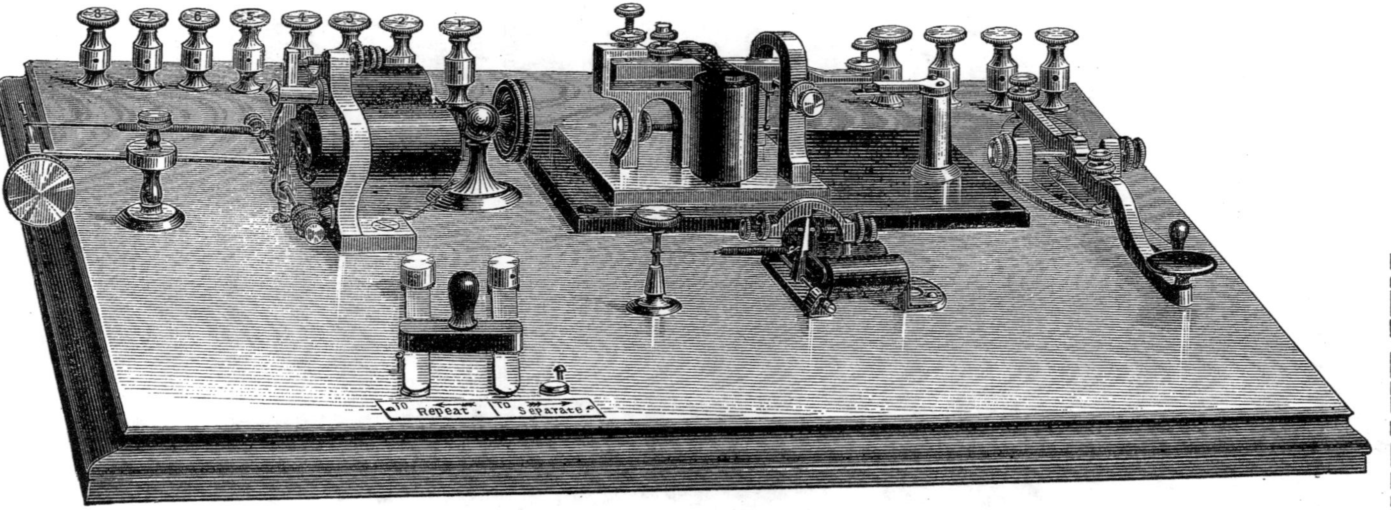

TILLOTSON'S AUTOMATIC REPEATER,

Price Complete, $125 00.

This Repeater consists of two Combination Sets, each exactly like the above Cut.

It is the simplest, easiest understood and most reliable Repeater in its adjustment and operation, of any yet devised.

To connect this Repeater for operation, consists simply in attaching the Main and Local Wires to the usual posts, as in any Morse Combination Set, and then connecting 8 wires from the numbered binding posts on one instrument *to the same numbers* on the other, so that a mistake in running wires is impossible, even to the most inexperienced operator.

When not in use, Repeating, the switches are turned and the instruments serve as Complete Combination sets for their respective lines.

This is the only Repeater yet introduced which is so easily managed and so simple as to be suitable for practical use in any Railway office.

SOUNDERS.

NEW GIANT SOUNDERS, PERFECTED.

[J H. BUNNELL'S PATENT, JULY 31, 1874.]

Beautiful in appearance, highly finished and put up in the most durable and substantial shape. They give enormous sound, with but very little local battery power. Hundreds of them are used in Railway and Commercial Telegraph offices, and all operators agree that no better Sounder is desired.

The great popularity of these Sounders has brought into the market cheaply constructed imitations of different degrees of worthlessness.

Buy direct from the manufacturers, L. G. Tillotson & Co., 5 & 7 Dey Street, New York, and you will get the best.

Price.. $7 50

INSTRUMENTS.

Sounders.

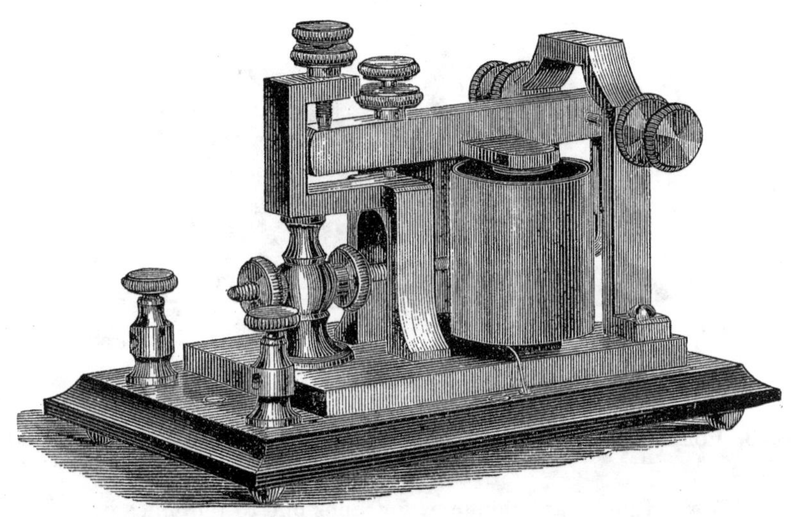

No. 1, Railroad $8 00

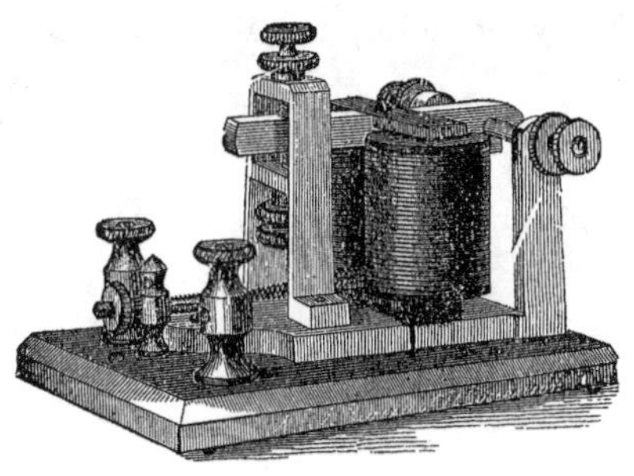

No. 2, Pony $6 50

INSTRUMENTS.

Sounders.

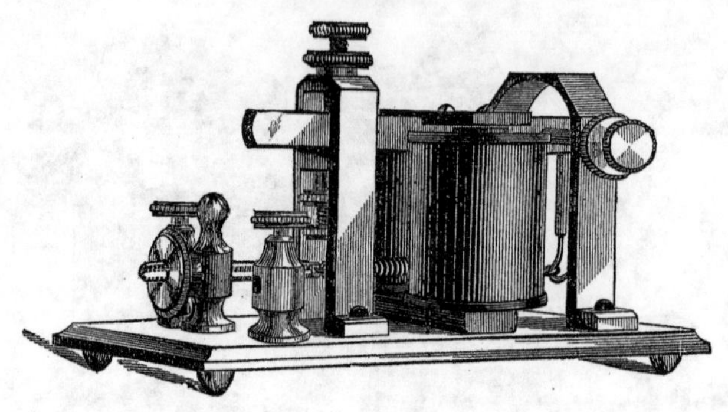

No. 3, Pony...$5 50

" 1, Main Line Giant Sounder, for lines one to ten miles in length...8 50

" 1, Main Line Railroad Sounder for lines one to ten miles.. 9 50

" 2, " " Pony Sounder, for lines one to ten miles in length...7 00

" 1, Repeating Sounder, plain points..............................10 00

" 1, " " spring " 11 00

INSTRUMENTS.

Sounders.

Western Union, New Style ; Nickel Plated Base..............$10 00

KEYS.

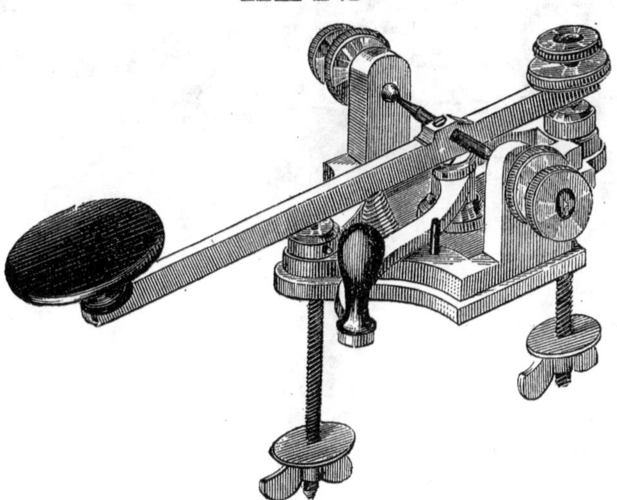

No. 1, Caton Pattern, Straight Lever..........................$6 50

INSTRUMENTS.

Keys.

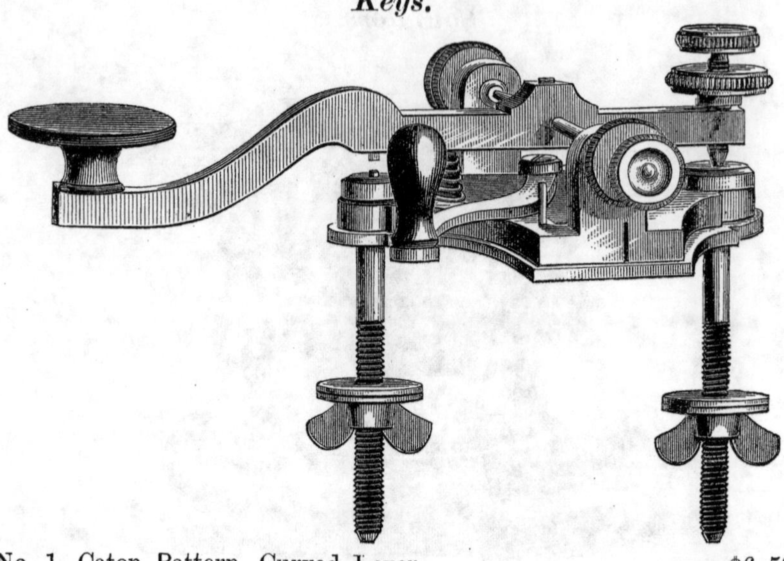

No. 1, Caton Pattern, Curved Lever... ....$6 50

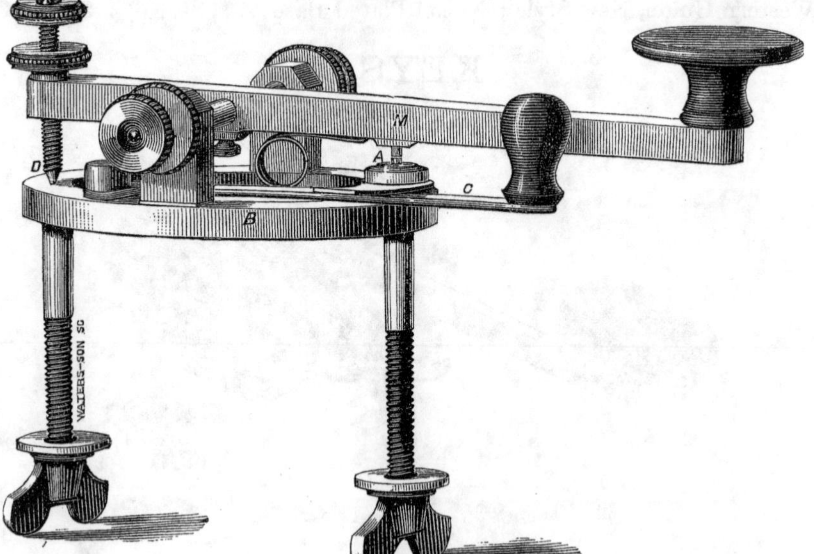

No. 2, Western Union Pattern, Straight Lever... ....$5 50
No. 2, " " " Curved " 5 50

INSTRUMENTS.

Keys.

No. 3, Curved Lever	$5 00
" 4, Straight Lever	4 00
" 4, Curved Lever	4 25

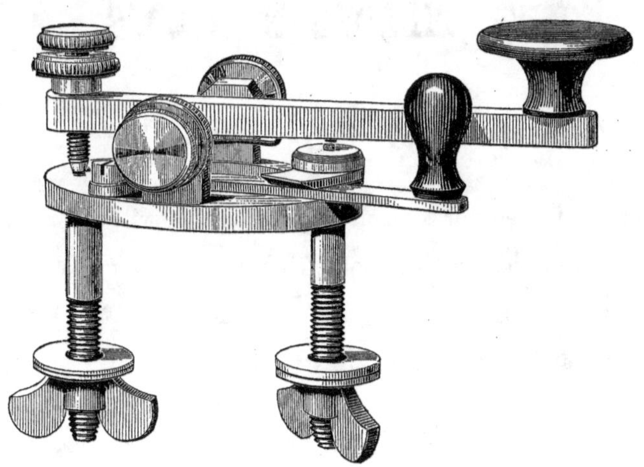

No. 5, Straight Lever	$3 25
" 5, Curved Lever	3 50
Key Springs, per doz	60

New!

Beautiful!!

Perfect!!!

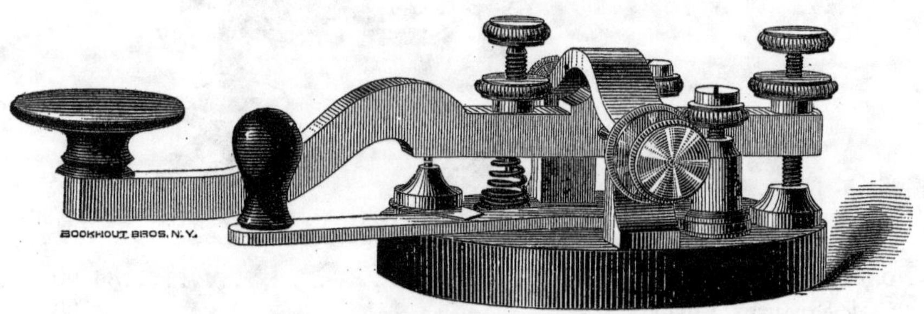

L. G. TILLOTSON & CO.'S

Improved Top Connection Key.

Can be connected for use on Desk or Table without mutilating the wood work or cutting large holes, as are required for other Keys. Has highly finished Hard Rubber Base, and is without exception the most beautiful and perfect Morse Key yet introduced.

Price $5.00.

CUT-OUTS.

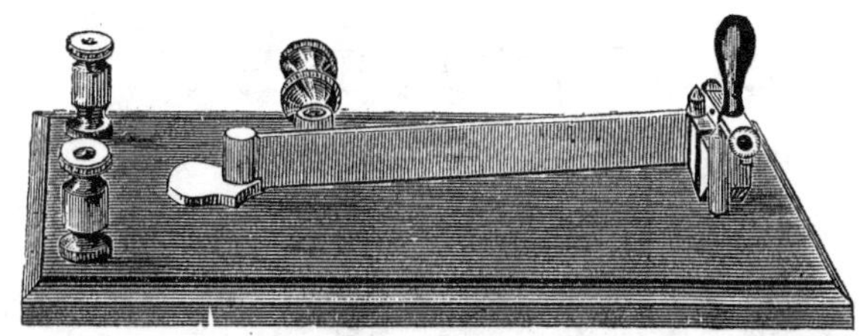

Cut-out, with plug, Single..............................$3 00
Cut-out, with plug, Double............................... 6 00

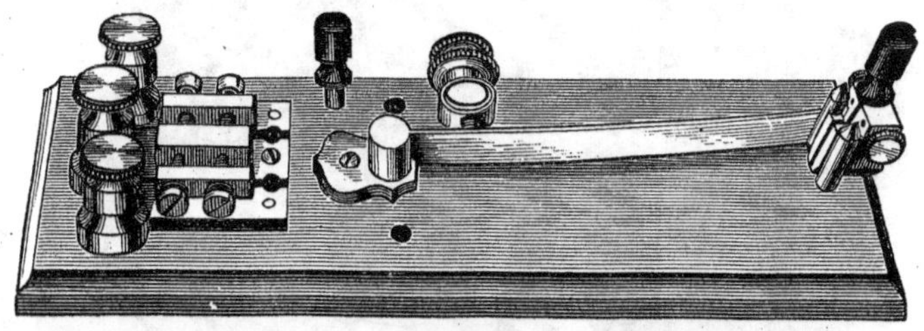

Cut-out, with plug, Lightning Arrester and Ground Switch.....$5 50
Cut-out, Peg, with Lightning Arrester and Ground Wire Switch. 5 50

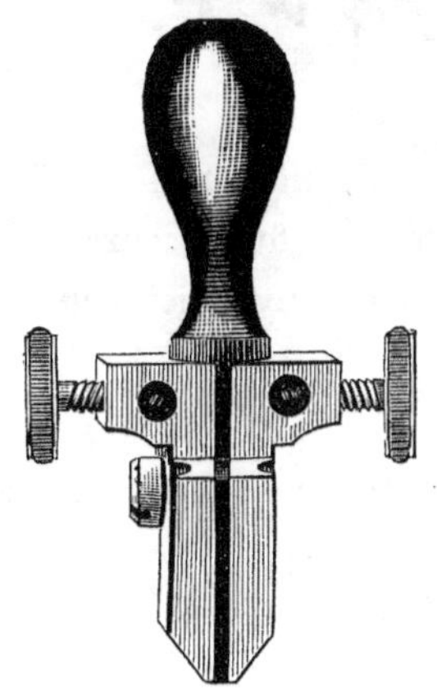

Plugs for Cut-outs..............................$1 00
Pegs " " 40

INSTRUMENTS.

GALVANOMETERS.

Standard Differential Galvanometer, adapted to requirements of Line and Battery tests, and all fine, accurate measurement of resistances, with rheostat to measure any resistance from one-one hundredth of an ohm upward.

Price Galvanometer and Rheostat in finely finished Mahogany
Traveling cases.......... .... $175 00
Galvanometer in traveling case 110 00
Rheostat, 1 to 10,000 ohms, in traveling case 70 00

INSTRUMENTS

Galvanometers.

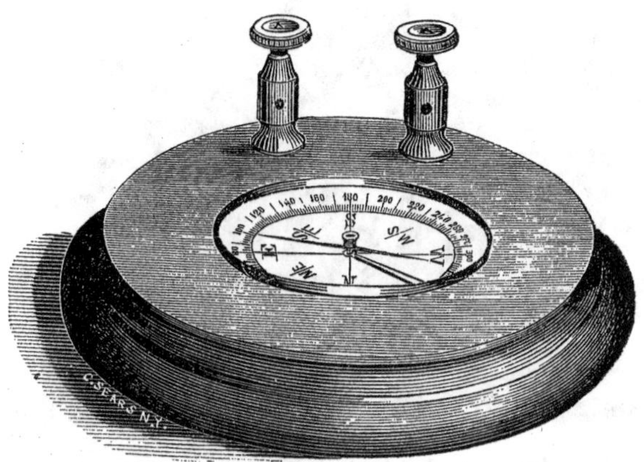

Horizontal.................................... $4 50 and $7 00
Perpendicular, under glass shade.................... 16 00 " 20 00
To order any desired Pattern.................................

[We furnish our instruments NICKEL PLATED for 20 per cent. additional to the list price.]

SWITCHES.

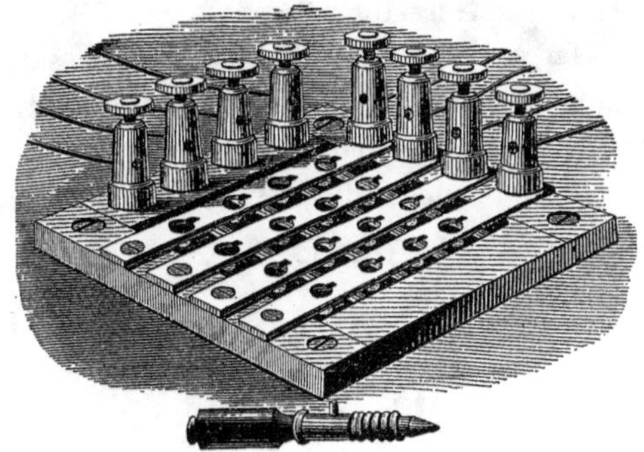

JONES' PATENT LOCK SWITCH, with Lightning Arrester.

Prices same as Western Union Pin Switches.

Extra plugs each.................................... 75

Switches.

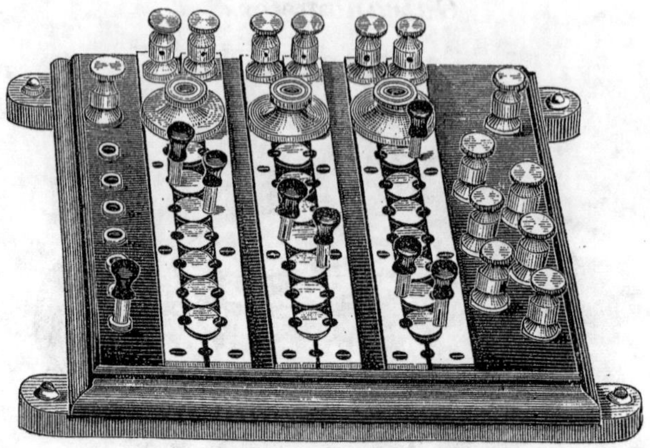

Western Union Pin Switches, with Improved Disc Lightning Arresters.

These Switches are now regarded as a standard article, having been generally adopted by the Western Union Telegraph Company and many other Corporations having extensive systems of wires.

Our improvement in the Lightning Arresters adds much to their beauty, practical merit and convenience—giving more perfect protection from severe lightning discharges, with less liability to make ground connections at the Arrester.

In ordering for large offices it will only be necessary to give the number and changes of wires, loops, batteries, and instruments to be provided for. We have unusual facilities for the prompt and perfect construction of Switches to meet all the requirements of large offices.

PRICES.

1 Wire, Way, 2 perpendicular Bars	$ 5 50
2 " " 4 " "	11 00
3 " " 6 " "	17 00
4 " " 8 " "	23 00
5 " " 10 " "	30 00
Over 10 Bars to order.	
Extra Pins, each	40

INSTRUMENTS.

Switches.

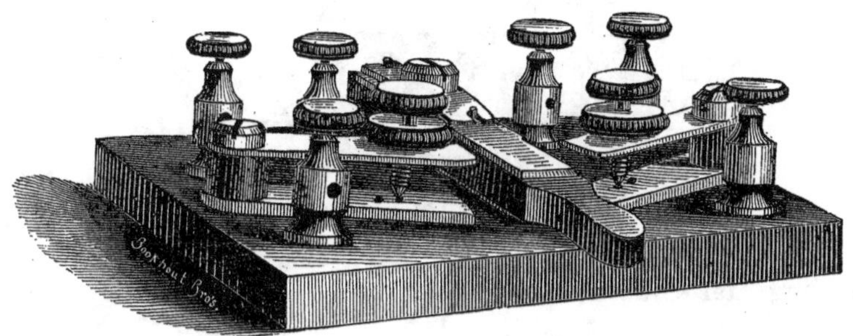

L. G. TILLOTSON & CO.'S QUICK SWITCH.

PRICE $7.50.

This is one of the most useful and perfect Switches ever devised. It is equally good as a *Button Repeater Switch,* as an *Instrument Switch.* for throwing a single instrument into either one of two lines by one movement of the lever without making the slighest break in either circuit, and as a *Cut-Out Switch* in the place of the ordinary Plug Cut-Out.

Local Circuit Changer... ....$3 00 to $4 00

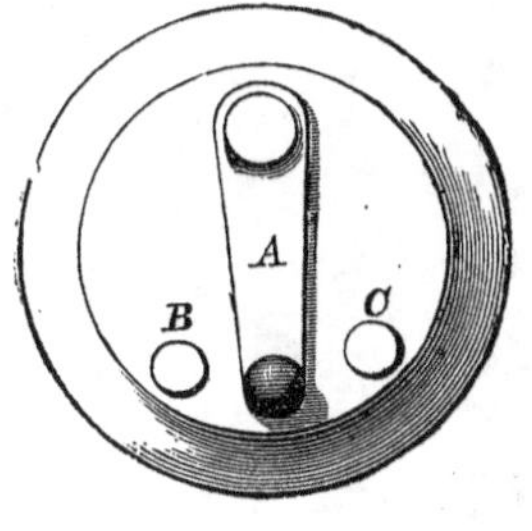

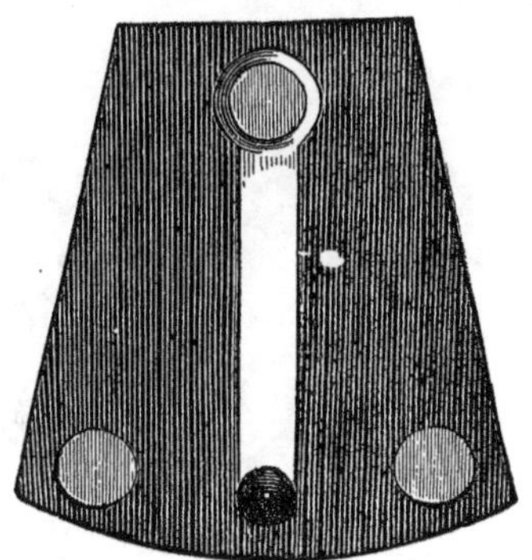

Circular Wood Base, 1 and 2 points......................$1 00
" " " 3 and 4 " 1 25
Battery or Ground Switch, Hard Rubber Base............... 1 25
Single point Switch " " " 1 00

Switches.

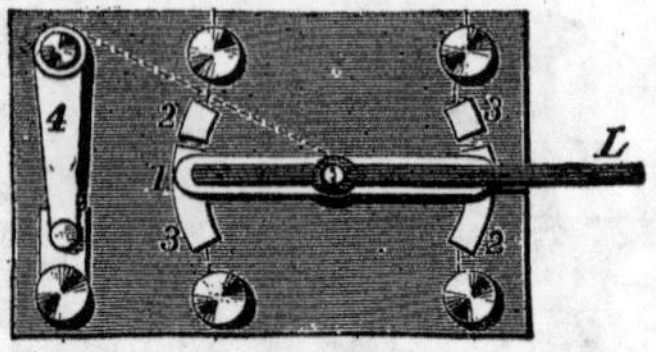

Repeating, Hard Rubber Base.................................. $6 00

Culgan, 1 to 5 lines, per perpendicular bar $3 00

Telephone Switches, complete with Bells or Annunciators, from $5 00 per Line upward.

LIGHTNING ARRESTERS.

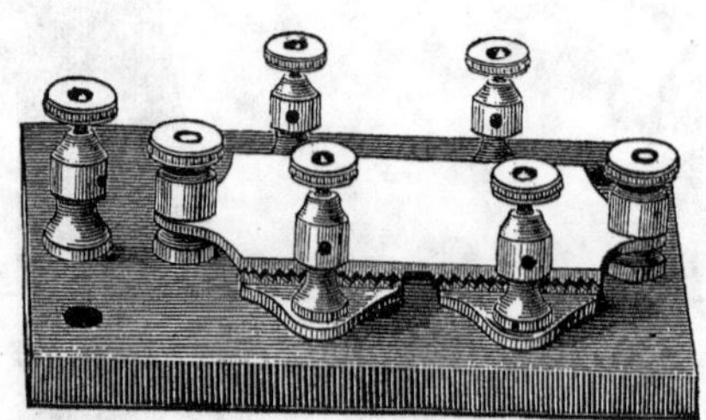

No. 1, With Heavy Plates $3 50
" 2, Disc Pattern 1 50
Globe Pattern.. 4 00
Cable, with platina points and wire.................$2 50 and 4 00

INSTRUMENTS.

Printing Telegraph Instrument $100 00

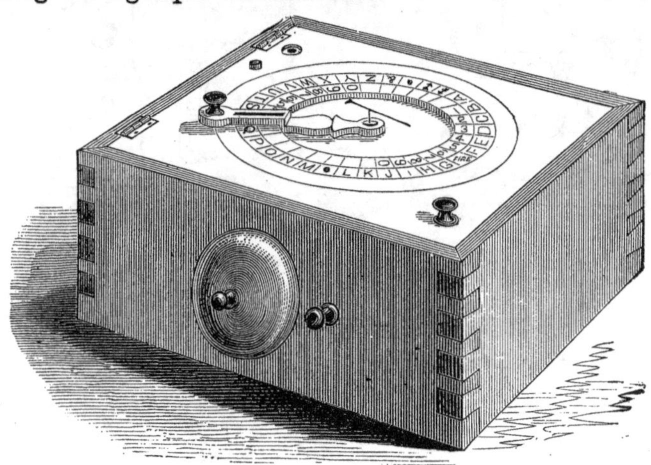

Alphabetical Dial Instrument $60 00

Instrument Materials, Parts of Instruments, Magnets, Binding Posts, &c.

Bases .... $0 50 to $2 00

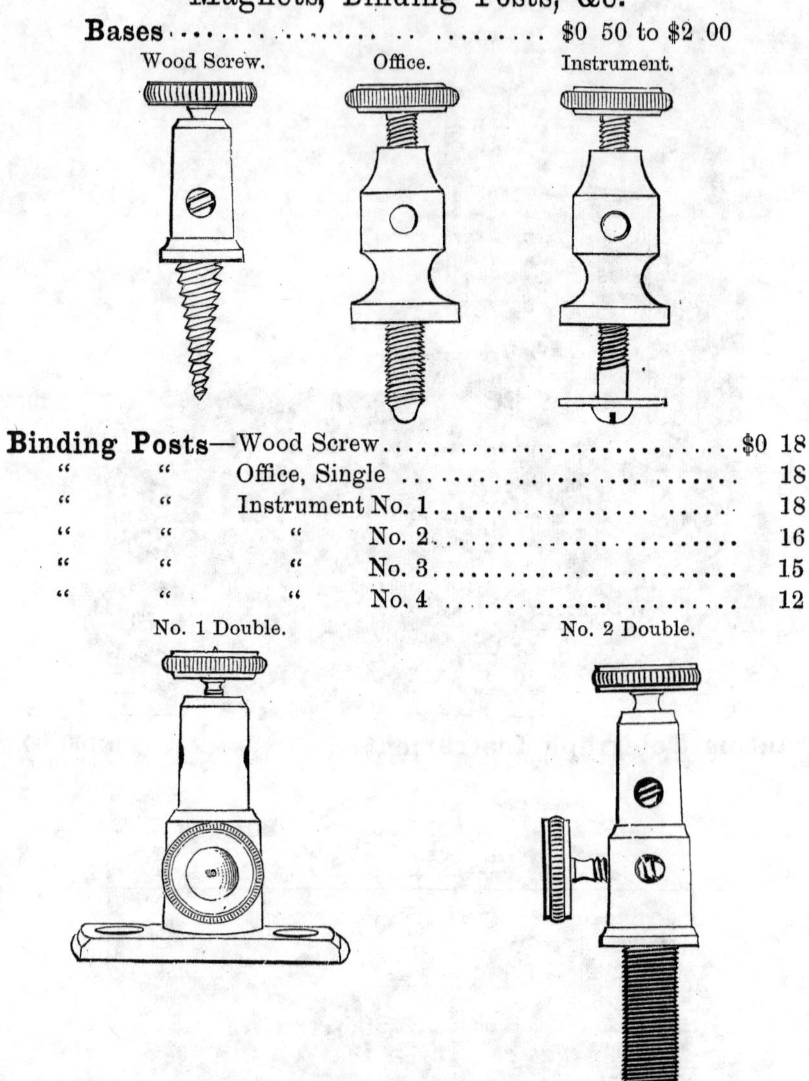

Binding Posts—Wood Screw.............................$0 18
" " Office, Single 18
" " Instrument No. 1.............................. 18
" " " No. 2.............................. 16
" " " No. 3.............................. 15
" " " No. 4.............................. 12

Binding Posts—Double, No. 1.............................$0 35
" " " No. 2, with wood screw.............. 30

INSTRUMENT MATERIALS.

Platinum—Sheet per dwt. 60 cts. Per oz. Market Price.

PLATINUM WIRE.

No. 12 Per inch	$ 80		No. 26 Per foot	$ 60
" 14 " "	50		" 28 " "	50
" 16 " "	35		" 30 " "	30
" 18 " "	25		" 32 " "	20
" 20 " "	20		" 34 " "	15
" 22 " "	15		" 36 " "	10
" 24 " "	08		" 40 " "	06

Nos. 12 to 22 pr. dwt 60
Nos. 24 to 30 " 75

Platinum Wire per oz. Market Price.

Watch Oil—For Registers, per bottle 25
Lacquer—Per bottle 50c., $1 00, $2 00
Adjustment Screws 10
" " **Check-Nuts** 10
Trunnion Screws 12
" " **Check-Nuts** 10
Key Lever Knobs 20
" " " **with dowels** 25
Circuit Closer Knobs 10
" " " **with dowels** 15
Top Screws for Binding Posts 08
Iron Screws " " " 01
Brass Washers 02
Instrument Springs—Each 10
" " per doz 60
Hard Rubber—In Sheets pr. lb 1 75
" " " Rods " 2 00
Tin Foil—(pure Imported) for Condensers, Sheets 12 x 36 inches, per sheet 10
Per doz. sheets 1 00
Per package of 24 sheets 1 50

ELECTRO MAGNETS.

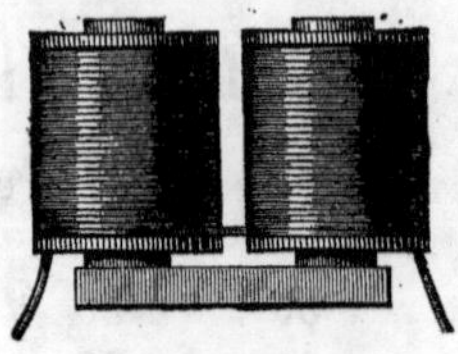

No. 1 Pony Sounder Size		$3 50
" 2 and 3 Pony Sounder size		2 75
No. 1 Light Relay size, 50 to 100 ohms		7 50
" 1 Standard " " 100 to 160 "		8 00
" 1 Heavy " " 100 to 400 "		9 00
" 2 Relay size 100 to 400 "		7 50
Pony " " 10 to 50 "		3 25

To order, any style.

PERMANENT MAGNETS.

Horseshoe, 2 inch	$0 10
" 2½ "	12
" 3 "	15
" 3½ "	20
" 4 "	25
" 4½ "	30
" 5 "	40
" 6 "	60
" 7 "	80
" 8 "	1 10
" 9 "	1 50
" 10 "	2 00
" 12 "	2 75
Magneto Machine Magnets, 4 inch	75
" " " 6 "	1 50
" " " 8 "	1 75
" " " 9 "	3 00
" " " 10 "	4 00

Special Magnets to order.

BATTERY MATERIAL.

HILL'S PATENT BATTERY.

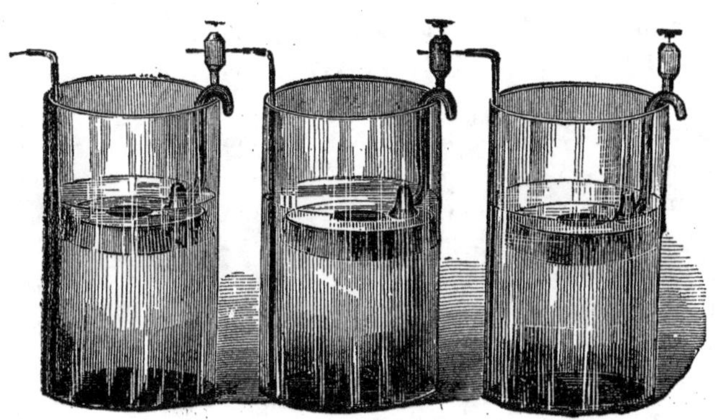

Main.—Hill's Patent.

No. 1, per cell	$1 25
Coppers	15
Hangers	20
Jars	45
Zincs	50
No. 2, per cell	1 40
Coppers	20
Hangers	20
Jars	50
Zincs	55

LOCAL.

Per cell	$1 60
Coppers	25
Hangers	20
Jars	50
Zincs	65

HILL BATTERY HANGER.

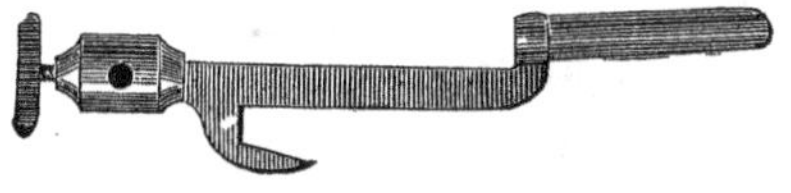

BATTERY MATERIAL.

Lockwood's Patent.

Per cell, complete	$2 50
Jars, 5x11 inches	60
Zincs	60
Zinc Supports	20
Zinc Connections	20
Coppers, Complete	90
Copper, Top Spiral	35
" Bottom Spiral	30
" Bolt and Nuts	20
" Insulated Wire	07

"Crow Foot" Gravity Battery.

Per cell, complete	$0 90
Jar, 6x8 inches	40
Zinc, with hanger and connector	35
Copper, complete	20

Callaud's Battery.

Same style as Western Union Gravity Battery, except that the zinc has a wire attached and is suspended from a wood strip crossing top of the jar.

MAIN.

Per cell, complete	$1 50
Coppers	25
Jars, $4\frac{5}{8}$x7	50
Zincs	55
Zinc Connector, with wood strip	20

LOCAL.

Per cell, complete	$1 60
Coppers	25
Jars	60
Zincs	60
Zinc Connector, with wood strip	20

GRAVITY BATTERY.

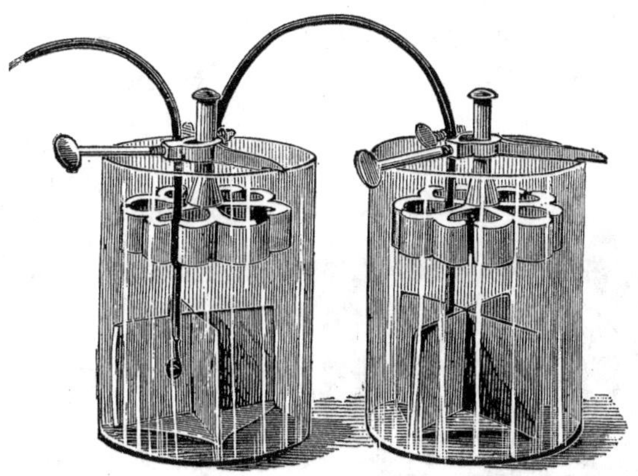

WESTERN UNION STANDARD WITH IMPROVED ADJUSTABLE ZINC HANGER AND CONNECTION.

No. 1, complete, (Western Union Main)	$1 50
Coppers	25
Jars, $4\frac{5}{8}$x7 inches	50
Zincs	50
Zinc Hangers	30
No. 2, complete	$1 60
Coppers	30
Jars, 6x8	55
Zincs	55
Zinc Hangers	35
No. 3, Same as No. 2, except Zincs, which are much larger	$1 85
Zincs	70
No. 4, (Western Union Local) Complete	$1 80
Coppers	30
Jars, $6\frac{1}{2}$x7	55
Zincs	65
Zinc Hangers	35

BATTERY MATERIAL.

THE WATSON BATTERY.

(Patented May 30, 1876.)

The Favorite Closed Circuit Battery for TELEPHONE EXCHANGE Circuits. The only BLUE VITRIOL Battery which DOES NOT REQUIRE ATTENTION.

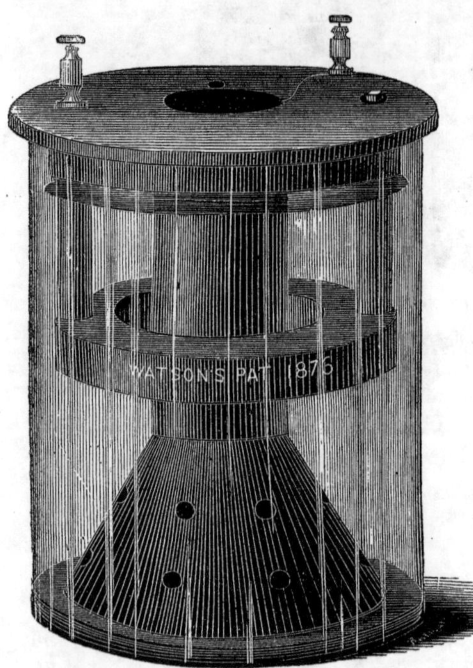

A new and great improvement over existing forms of Blue Vitriol Battery. Its chief merits are *strength in action*, being considerably stronger than Daniell's for use either as local or main battery; *Cleanliness*, being provided with a close cover, which also prevents evaporation of the liquids; *Convenience and simplicity*. The construction and operation of this Battery is such that it may be kept in perfect order with less labor and attention than any other, when it is either in active constant use, as in a telegraph office, or left on open circuit most of the time, as in the laboratory. All it requires is a supply of blue vitriol dropped into the top of the lead tube when it appears to require it.

It possesses every other merit which pertains to the best forms of Blue Vitriol Battery.

Directions.

Fill the Jar nearly two-thirds full with a mixture of one-quarter pound sulphate of zinc to two quarts of water. Then put the tube and zinc and cover in position as shown in the cut above, and drop into the tube at the top from one-half pound to three pounds of blue vitriol. If the Battery is not to be used very constantly, the lesser amount of blue vitriol will do, but if the battery is to be worked steadily, fill up the tube with blue vitriol.

Price, Complete Cell	$1 90
Jar (6x8 inches)	50
Zinc	50
Zinc Connections	15
Lead Negative with Connection	65
Cover, (Porcelain)	15

Eagles' Metallic Battery.

MAIN.

Round Cell, complete	$2 00
Lead Jars, each	1 30
Zincs, with wires attached	60
Iusulating Fenders	03

LOCAL.

Square Cell, complete	$2 25
Lead Jars, each	1 50
Zincs, with wires attached	65
Insulating Fenders	03

Other sizes than the above for special uses furnished to order.

GROVE BATTERY.

MAIN.

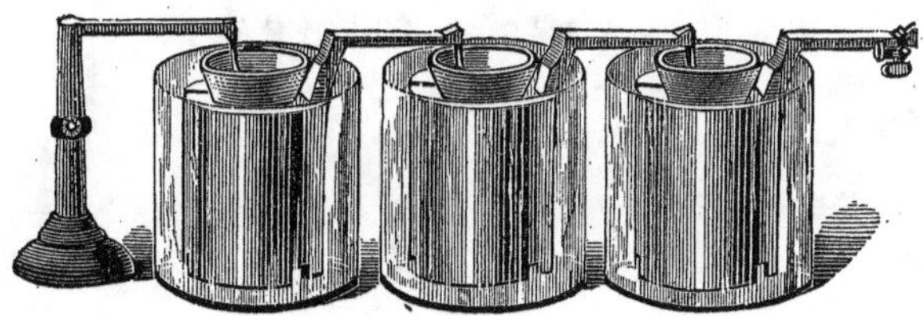

Per Cell, complete	$1 75
Platinum, small	80
" large	95
Porous Cups, per doz	1 25
" " each	15
Tumblers, per doz	3 50
" each	35
Zincs	50
Battery, Platinum Standards	75

BATTERY MATERIAL.

DANIELL'S BATTERY.

Per Cell, complete	$1 75
Coppers, with pockets	65
" shells	45
" pockets	25
Porous Cups, per doz., No. 1	2 00
" " each	20
Jars, Earthen	25
" Glass	60
" " per doz	6 00
Zincs	40
Zinc Clamps	20

BATTERY MATERIAL.

CARBON BATTERY

MAIN.

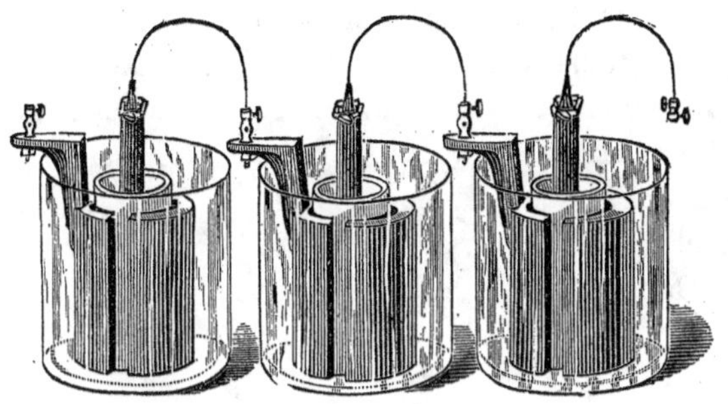

No. 1, per cell, complete	$1 75
" Carbons, Patent Connections	55
" " plain	18
" " Clamps	15
" " Connections (Platinum Faced)	25
Jars, per doz	3 50
" each	35
Porous Cups, per doz	1 25
" " each	15
Zincs	50
Zinc Connections	25
No. 1½, per cell, complete	2 25
" Carbons, plain	50
" " Clamps	20
" " Connections (Platinum Faced)	30
" Porous Cups, per doz	1 30
" " " each	15
Jars, per doz	3 50
Zincs	60
Zinc Connections	25

BATTERY MATERIAL.

Carbon Battery.—Continued.

No. 2, per cell, with Heavy Zinc, Complete	$4 50
" " " Rolled "	3 50
" Carbons	75
" " Clamps	30
" " Connections (Platinum-Faced)	50
" Zincs, Heavy	2 50
" " Rolled	1 25
" " Connections	25
" Jars, per doz	6 00
" " each	60
" Porous Cups, per doz	3 00
" " " each	30

CARBON PLATES FOR BUNSEN, GRENET, STOHRER, SMEE, AND OTHER BATTERIES.

$1\frac{3}{8}$	inches wide,	$4\frac{1}{4}$	inches long,	$\frac{1}{4}$	inch thick		$0 15
$1\frac{3}{8}$	"	$4\frac{3}{4}$	"	$\frac{1}{4}$	"		16
$1\frac{3}{4}$	"	$5\frac{3}{4}$	"	$\frac{1}{4}$	"		18
6	"	9	"	$\frac{1}{4}$	"		75
6	"	10	"	$\frac{1}{4}$	"		80
3	"	6	"	$\frac{1}{2}$	"		70
$4\frac{1}{2}$	"	7	"	$\frac{1}{2}$	"		80
$4\frac{1}{2}$	"	9	"	$\frac{5}{8}$	"		90
$\frac{7}{8}$	"	6	"	$\frac{5}{8}$	"		18
$1\frac{3}{4}$	"	6	'	$\frac{5}{8}$	"		50
2	"	9	"	$\frac{3}{4}$	"		75
9	"	12	"	$\frac{1}{2}$	"		2 25
10	"	12	"	$\frac{1}{2}$	"		2 25
12	"	12	"	$\frac{1}{2}$	"		2 50

Carbon Pencils, for Electric Light, $\frac{1}{4}$ inch square, 10 inches long	15
" " " " " $\frac{3}{8}$ inch square, 12 inches long	20

BATTERY MATERIAL.

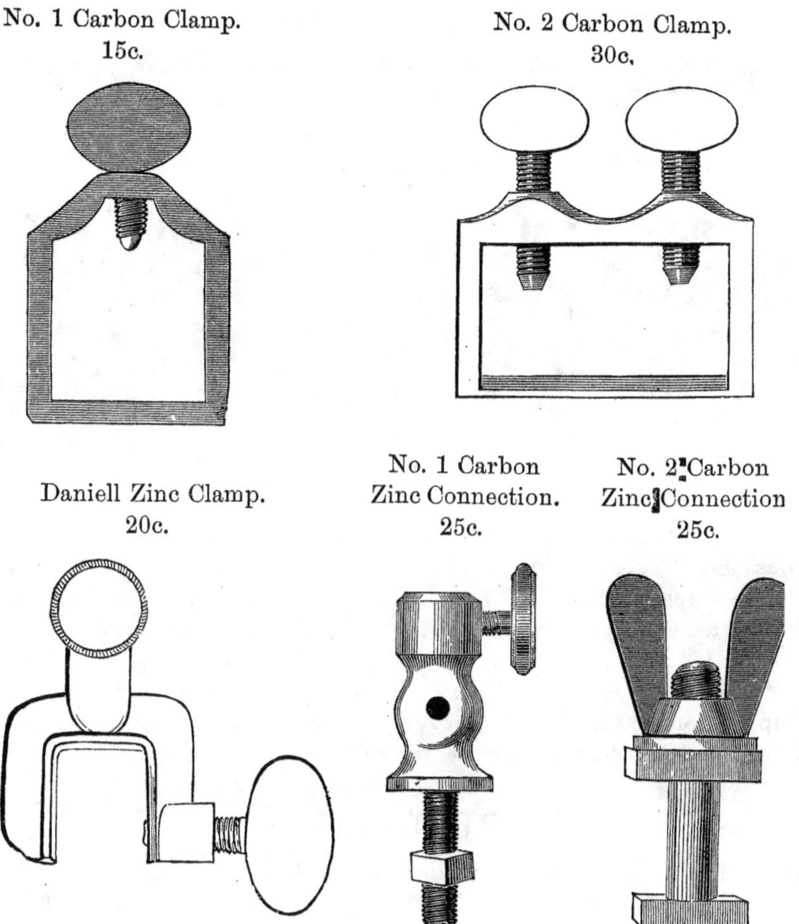

No. 1 Carbon Clamp. 15c.

No. 2 Carbon Clamp. 30c.

Daniell Zinc Clamp. 20c.

No. 1 Carbon Zinc Connection. 25c.

No. 2 Carbon Zinc Connection 25c.

FLUID FOR CARBON BATTERY.

Mix one gallon of sulphuric acid and three gallons of water. Then, in a separate vessel, dissolve six pounds bichromate of potash in two gallons of boiling water, mixing the whole thoroughly together. When cold it is ready for use.

Battery Material for Gold, Silver and Nickel Plating, Electric Light, Laboratory Purposes, etc.

THE IMPROVED

NITRO-CHROMIC BATTERY.

For Electroplating, Electro-Motors, or any other Purpose where Great Quantity of Electricity is required.

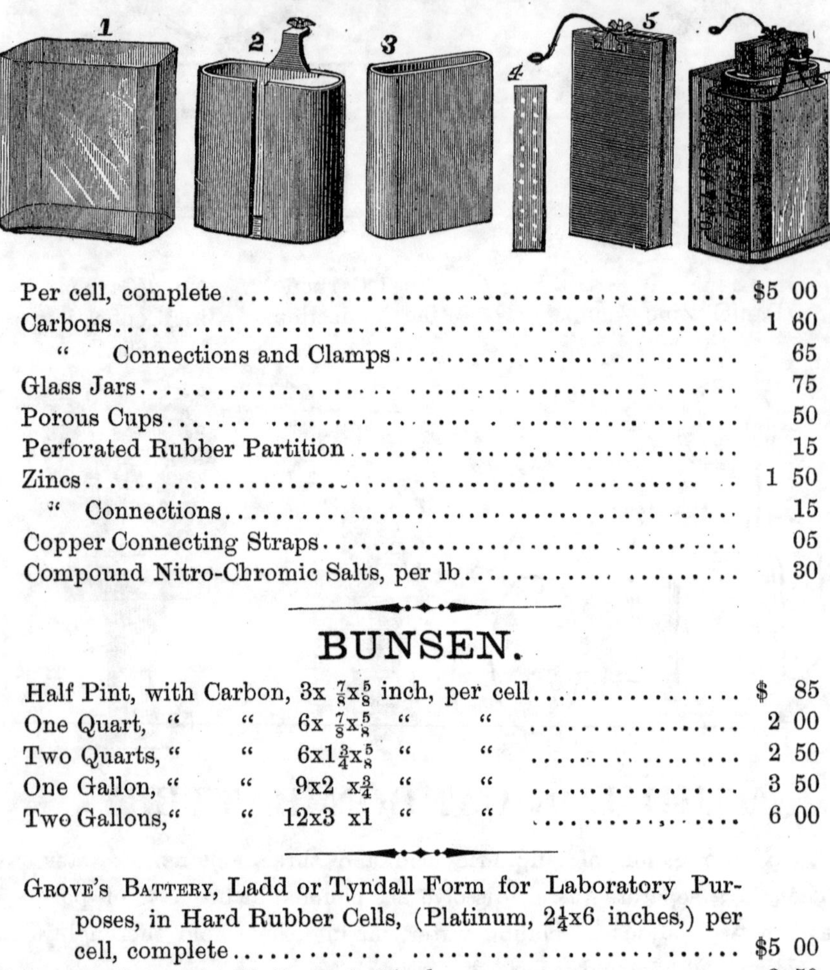

Per cell, complete	$5 00
Carbons	1 60
" Connections and Clamps	65
Glass Jars	75
Porous Cups	50
Perforated Rubber Partition	15
Zincs	1 50
" Connections	15
Copper Connecting Straps	05
Compound Nitro-Chromic Salts, per lb	30

BUNSEN.

Half Pint, with Carbon, 3x $\frac{7}{8}$x$\frac{5}{8}$ inch, per cell	$ 85
One Quart, " " 6x $\frac{7}{8}$x$\frac{5}{8}$ " "	2 00
Two Quarts, " " 6x1$\frac{3}{4}$x$\frac{5}{8}$ " "	2 50
One Gallon, " " 9x2 x$\frac{3}{4}$ " "	3 50
Two Gallons, " " 12x3 x1 " "	6 00

Grove's Battery, Ladd or Tyndall Form for Laboratory Purposes, in Hard Rubber Cells, (Platinum, 2$\frac{1}{4}$x6 inches,) per cell, complete	$5 00
Per cell Complete, Platinum 2x5 inches	3 50

BATTERY MATERIAL.

Smee, with Carbon Plate.

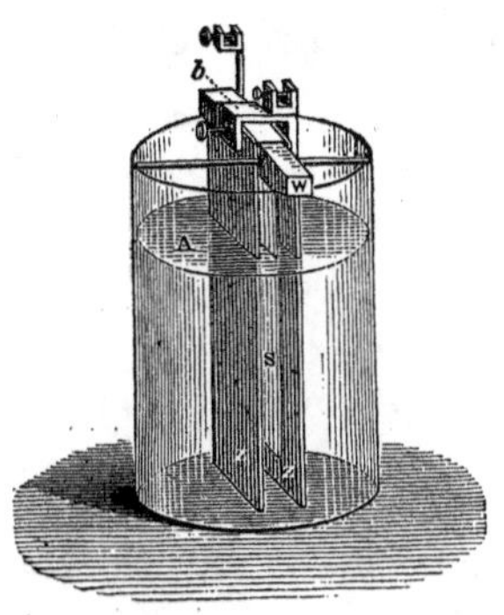

No. 1 (Zinc Plates 3½x4¾ inches), per cell	$2 85
" Jar	40
" Zincs (rolled), per pair	60
" Carbons and Connections	85
" Carbon Connector	18
" Carbon Washers	10
" Clamps	75
" Wood Supports	08
No. 2 (Zinc Plates 3½x7½ inches), per cell	3 25
" Jars	45
" Zincs (rolled), per pair	80
" Carbon and Connections	95
" Carbon Connectors	18
" Carbon Washers	10
" Clamps	75
" Wood Supports	08
No. 3 (Zinc Plates 4x8 inches), per cell	3 90
" Jars	60
" Zincs (rolled), per pair	1 00
" Carbon and Connections	1 25
" Carbon Connectors	18
" Carbon Washers	10
" Clamps	75
" Wood Supports	08

[ROLLED ZINC PLATES, the best in the market, per lb., 20c. Special price given for large quantity.]

BATTERY MATERIAL.

Smee with Carbon Plate.

No. 4, (Zinc plates 6x10 inches,) per cell	$5 50
" Jar	90
" Zincs (rolled,) per pair	1 50
" Carbon with Connections	2 00
" Carbon Connectors	18
" Carbon Insulator	10
" Clamps	75
" Wood Supports	10

The SILVER PLATINUM SMEE BATTERY is the same as the CARBON SMEE, except it has PLATINIZED SILVER PLATE in place of the CARBON. Prices complete.

No. 1, per cell	$4 00
" 2, "	4 75
" 3, "	6 00

Carbon with Connections for Electrotyping Baths.

9x10	inches	plain	connections	$3 25
10x12	"	"	"	3 75
10x12	"	laced	"	5 50
12x12	"	"	"	6 00

SOLUTION FOR AMALGAMATING ZINCS.

Mix 1 lb. nitric with 2 lbs. hydrochloric acid, and add 8 ozs. mercury. When the mercury is dissolved, add 3 lbs. more hydrochloric acid. To amalgamate the zinc, immerse it in this solution for one or two seconds, then remove it quickly to a dish of clean water, and rub it with a brush or a cloth, when it will be found covered with a fine, even coat of mercury. This solution can be kept in a covered jar, and used many times.

The Leclanché Battery.

THE ONLY PERFECT BATTERY FOR ALL OPEN CIRCUIT WORK.

[Secured by Letters Patent in the United States.]

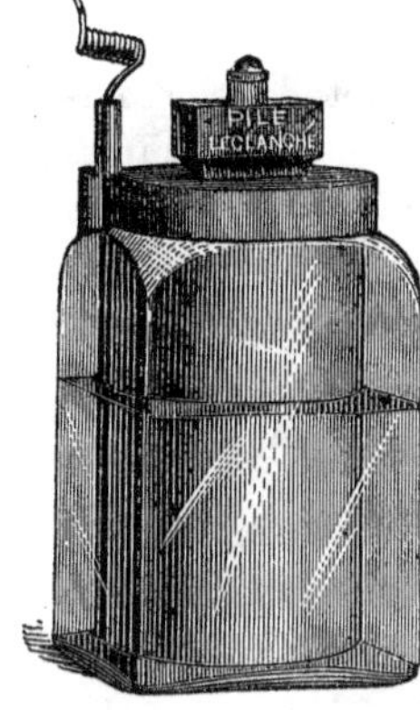

ADOPTED BY TELEPHONE COMPANIES AS THE ONLY PERFECT BATTERY FOR OPERATING TELEPHONE TRANSMITTERS.

It is the ONLY BATTERY WHICH WILL GIVE SATISFACTION in operating HOUSE and HOTEL ANNUNCIATORS and BURGLAR ALARMS, and is adopted by EVERY MANUFACTURER of FIRST-CLASS HOUSE and HOTEL ELECTRIC BELL SYSTEMS IN THE WORLD as the ONLY RELIABLE BATTERY FOR POPULAR USE.

Some of its advantages may be enumerated as follows :

Running expenses reduced to a minimum.
The entire absence of acids.
Its great cleanliness and entire absence of odor.
Impossibility of getting out of order,
Does not freeze.
Will last without renewal from one month to several years, according to use, at the end of which time the porous cells can be renewed at a moderate expense.

PRICE LIST

DISQUE. Size, 4½ inches by 6 inches.		No. 1. Size, 3½ inches by 6 inches.		No. 2. Size, 3 inches by 5 inches.	
Porous Cell	$1 75	Porous Cell	$1 55	Porous Cell	$1 40
Jar	20	Jar	18	Jar	15
Zinc, Amalgamated	12	Zinc, Amalgamated	12	Zinc, Amalgamated	12
Sal Ammoniac	8	Sal Ammoniac	5	Sal Ammoniac	3
Complete Element	$2 00	Complete Element	$1 80	Complete Element	$1 65
" " Seal'd	2 20	" " Seal'd	2 00	" " Seal'd	1 80

SAL AMMONIAC, 20 CENTS PER POUND.

A Liberal Discount to the Trade.

L. G TILLOTSON & CO.,

Sole Agents for the Leclanché Battery.

The Grenet Battery.

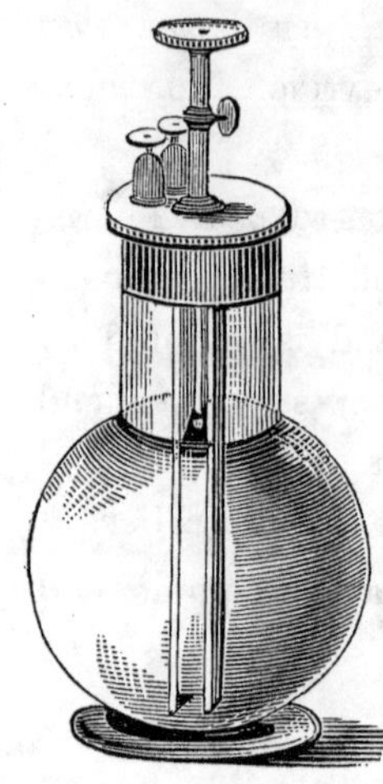

This Battery is especially adapted for experimental and illustrative purposes. It occupies but little space, furnishes an immense quantity of current, is beautiful in design, and, as the zinc can be raised from the fluid, may be kept charged, ready for use, for many months, and can be set in action any time when required, by simply depressing the brass rod which slides through the centre of the cover of the cell, and to which the zinc is attached.

For operating Induction coils and Electro-Medical Instruments it is unequalled.

No. 1, 6 inches high		$2 50
" 2, 8 "		4 50
" 3, 10 "		5 50
" 4, 12 "		6 50
" 5, 12 "	Double Zincs and Carbons	12 00
Extra Zincs, Nos. 1 and 2		25
" " " 3 " 4		30

DIRECTIONS.

To Make the Solution.—To three pints of cold water add five fluid ounces of sulphuric acid ; when this becomes cold, add six ounces (or as much as the solution will dissolve) of finely pulverized bi-chromate of potassa. Mix well.

To Charge the Battery.—Pour the above solution into the glass cell until it nearly reaches the top of the spherical part, then draw up the zinc, and place the elements in the cell. The fluid should not quite reach the zinc when it is drawn up.

CHEMICALS and METALS.

Acid, Nitric.—(41 degrees,) per lb., lowest market price	
" **Sulphuric** " " " "	
" **Hydrochloric** " " " "	
Bichromate Potash	30
Bisulphate of Mercury—per lb	$1 50
Chloride of Ammonia—per lb	20
Bichloride of Platinum—per oz	1 00
Fluid—(for Carbon Battery), per lb	10
Blue Vitriol—per lb., small packages	10
" " " by bbl., lowest market price	
Quicksilver—per lb	80
" " in flasks, lowest market price	
Sulphate of Zinc—per lb	10
Subject to fluctuations of the market	
Zinc Plates—(rolled), per lb	20
Special prices for large quantities.	

BATTERY UTENSILS.

Brushes, per doz.—No. 1	$5 00
" " " " 2	4 00
Funnels—Gutta Percha	50c. to 1 50
" Glass	30
Glass Strips	$
Insulators—Battery	40
" " Robertson's Patent	30
Stands—To order, any size	
Syringes—No. 6	2 50
" Extra Pipes, each	50
" " Valves, each	30
Hydrometers for Hill and Callaud Battery	50
Acidometers	1 25

Instruments, Batteries and Materials,

Especially adapted to the requirements of *Learners of Telegraphy*, *Schools*, *Colleges*, and the operation of *all Short Telegraph Lines.*

The Home Learners' Instrument.

[Pat. May 1st, 1877.]

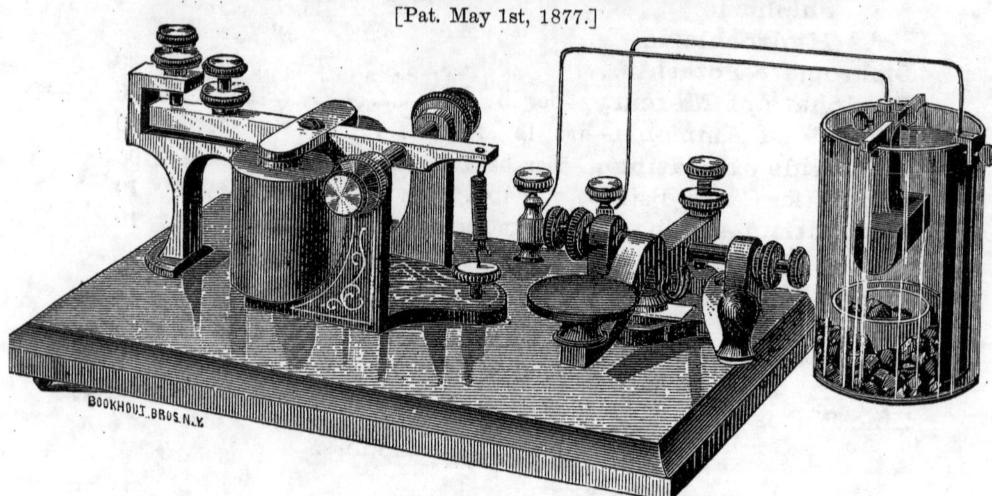

A complete and perfect sounder and key combined, on mahogany base, including Battery, Chemicals, Wire, Book of Instruction, and everything necessary for a FIRST-CLASS TELEGRAPH Outfit for the Student's use, for practice at home, or for operating ALL SHORT LINES OF TELEGRAPH.

Description.—The above cut is a correct representation of the instrument as it is furnished, ready for use.

The Sounder is a modified pattern of the celebrated Giant Sounder.

The Key is of medium size, with curved lever of the celebrated Caton Pattern.

The Battery is an improved form of Gravity Cell, equal in power to the largest sized, best Western Union Gravity Battery.

The ***Book of Instruction*** is the latest edition of the well-known standard work, entitled ***Smith's Manual of Telegraphy***.

With the Outfit is also included chemicals and wire for setting up and operating the instruments, for practising or communicating purposes.

Complete outfit	$4 50
Instruments, without Battery	3 80
" " " wound with finer wire, for lines one to fifteen miles	4 50
Little Giant Battery, per cell	65
Zincs, each	20
Negative Plate	10
Connecting Clamp	10
Zinc Hanger	05
Glass Jar	20

Metallic Base Learners' Instrument.

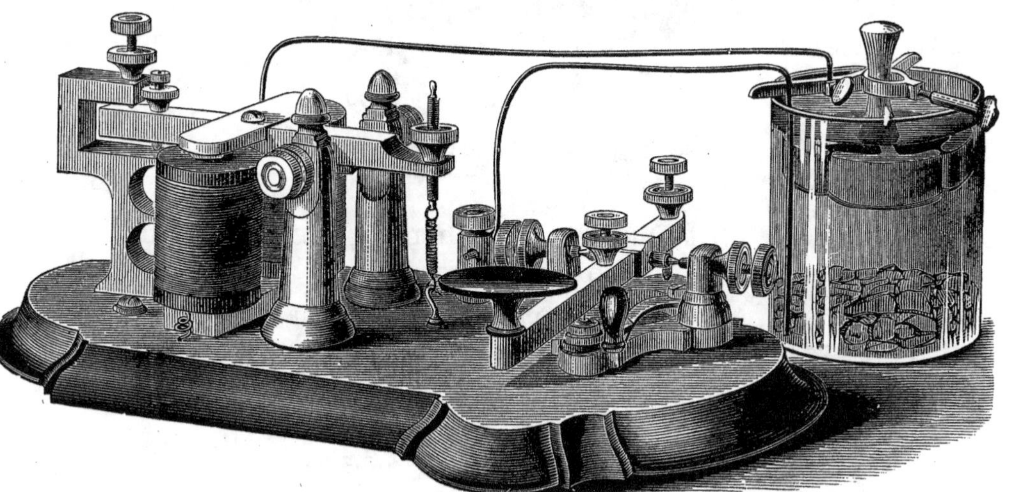

Complete and Perfect full sized Sounder and Key combined, with Book of Instruction, Battery, Wire, and all Necessary Materials.

Since the introduction of these Instruments, five years since, NINE THOUSAND sets have been sold and put in operation throughout the country, giving perfect satisfaction to everybody.

These sets are made in the best manner, and are just exactly the thing wanted for Learners' Use, for Telegraph Schools, or for Short Lines, from a few feet to twelve miles long.

Learners' Instrument complete, with Battery, Book of Instructions, Wire and all necessary Materials to put in operation, singly or on a Short Line.............................$6 75
Learners' Instrument without Battery, etc.................................. 5 20
Ornamental Learners' Instrument, Rubber covered Coils, etc.................................. 6 00
Extra Battery, (No. 1 Gravity, page 79)..................................per cell 1 00

Same Instruments wound with finer wire, so as to operate satisfactorily lines up to 12 miles in length, $1.00 in addition to the above prices.

Learners' Sounders and Keys on Separate Bases.

Same style as shown in cut of Learners' Instrument.

Learners' Sounders...$2 80
Learners' Sounders, with rubber-covered coils.. 3 20
Learners' Keys, fine finish,.. 2 40

Excelsior Cut-Out with Lightning Arrester, and Ground Switch.

This is an excellent and complete combination at a very low price answering all of the above purposes in connection with amateur telegraphy. Price, $1.50.

LINE MATERIAL.

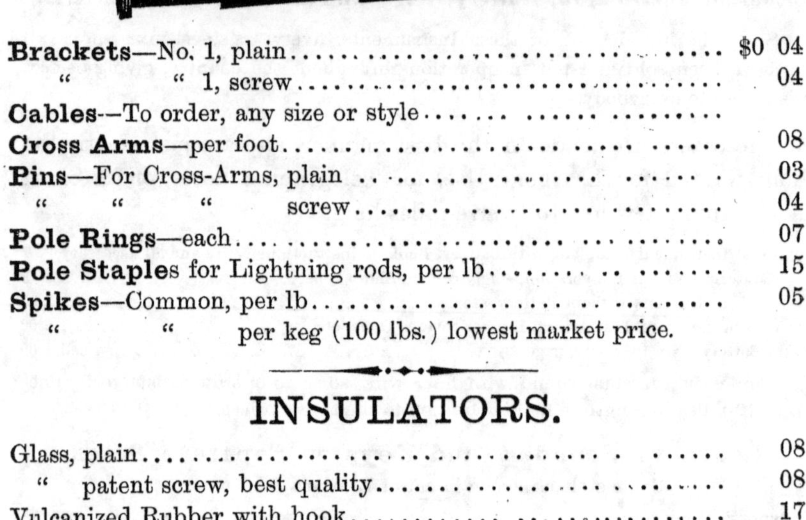

Brackets—No. 1, plain	$0 04
" " 1, screw	04
Cables—To order, any size or style	
Cross Arms—per foot	08
Pins—For Cross-Arms, plain	03
" " " screw	04
Pole Rings—each	07
Pole Staples for Lightning rods, per lb	15
Spikes—Common, per lb	05
" " per keg (100 lbs.) lowest market price.	

INSULATORS.

Glass, plain	08
" patent screw, best quality	08
Vulcanized Rubber with hook	17
Kenosha, with pin or Bracket	

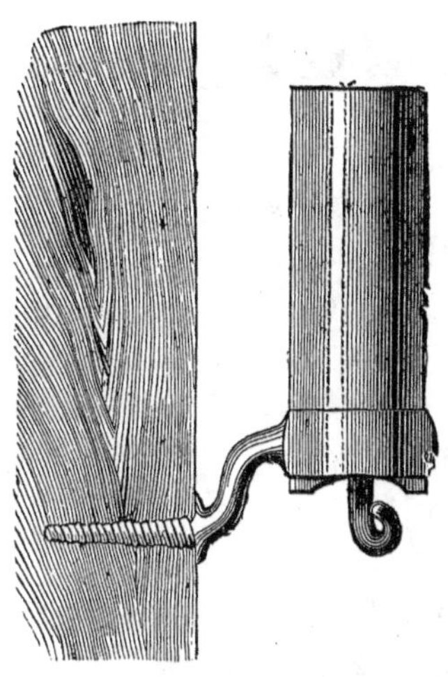

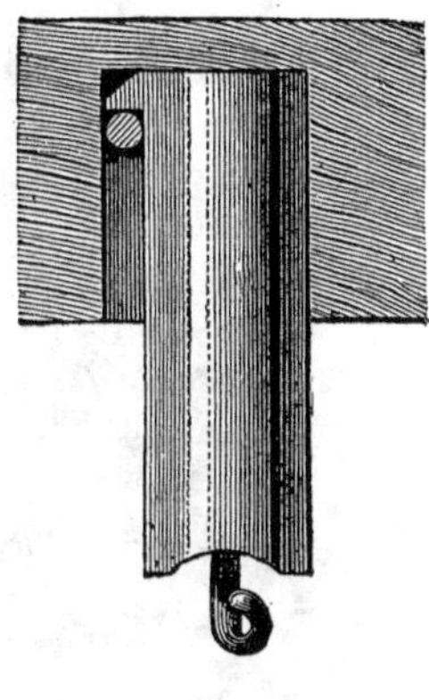

Brook's Patent Paraffine Insulator.

L. G. TILLOTSON & CO., SOLE AGENTS.

Price of Insulator with Screw Shank	$0 38
" " for Cross Arms..............................	30

THE LA BASTIE
Bottle Insulator, Patented.

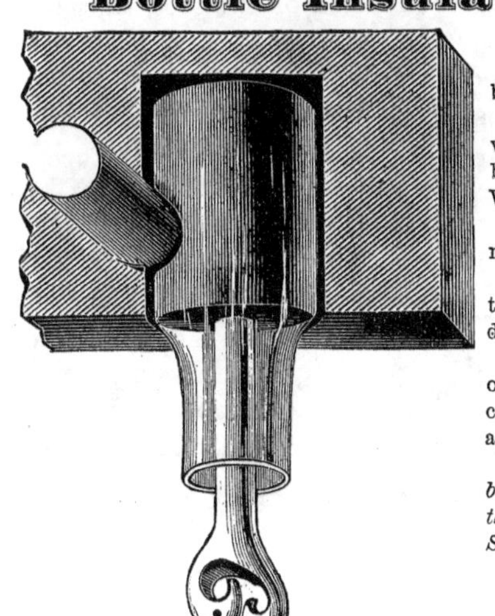

The advantages of this Insulator are:

1st. It exceeds ordinary Insulators a *thousand fold* by actual measurement in its insulating properties.

2d. It has an easy fastening for any size of wire, without bending or straining the latter, and cannot be displaced or broken by any strain which the wire Will bear.

3d. It costs less than any other Insulator of equal merit.

The glass shell is made of the celebrated La Bastie toughened glass, and in its present shape is as durable as iron.

As the light penetrates freely to the inner chamber of the Insulator, *insects will not harbor in it.* A common cause of defective insulation is thus aAoided.

As a cross arm Insulator, this form is not only better than any ever yet devised, but it is cheaper than ordinary glass and pin. Price 12 *cents each Special rates for quantities.*

L. G. TILLOTSON & CO.,

GENERAL AGENTS.

THE IMPROVED
Glass Screw Insulator.

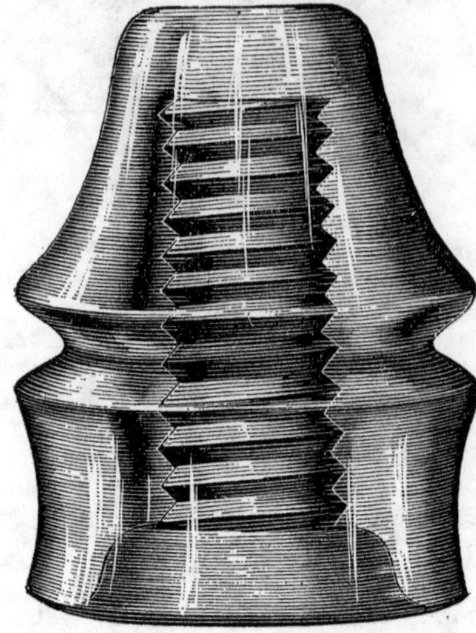

Patented:

Jan'y 25th, 1865. Re-issue Feb'y [22d, 1870.
Jan'y 25th, 1870.
May 31st, 1870.
April 4th, 1871.
Sept. 10th, 1872.
May 4th, 1875.
July 11th, 1871.
June 25th, 1872.
July 16th, 1872.
May 8th, 1877.
March 20th, 1877.

The superiority of the Patent Screw Glass Insulator over all others is thoroughly acknowledged by all who are interested in Telegraphy, and needs no recommendation, beyond a mere mention of the fact, that it is now in general use in this and other countries. The right to manufacture Screw Glass Insulators is vested exclusively in the Owners of the above named Letters Patent, whose Sole Agents we are, and all persons are hereby cautioned against engaging in the manufacture, sale or use of Screw Glass Insulators, without authority, as legal proceedings will be instituted in case of any infringement upon the above-mentioned Letters Patent.

PRICES:

Screw Glass Insulator, full size, *Regular Pattern*	$0 08
" " " " " *W. U. Pattern*	08
" " " Pony "	04

The trade supplied on favorable terms.

L. G. TILLOTSON & CO., Sole Agents,
5 & 7 Dey Street, New York.

THE PONY

Screw Glass Insulator,

(PATENTED.)

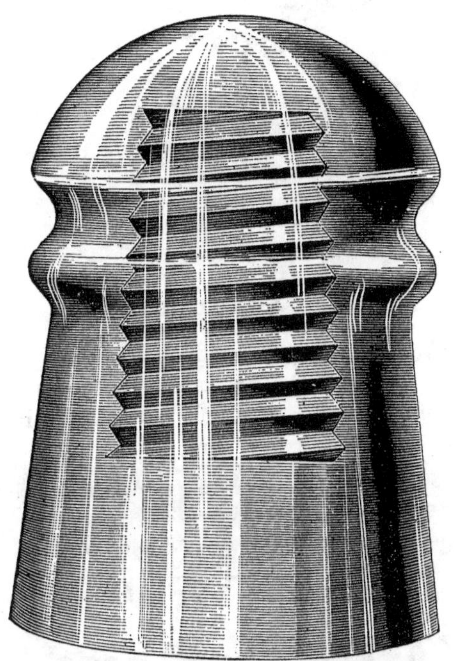

Especially adapted to TELEPHONE and PRIVATE LINE CONSTRUCTION.

This new style Insulator is used by the various TELEPHONE COMPANIES, and is particularly recommended as being the most perfect Insulator for all wires from No. 18 to No. 11.

The above cut shows full size and they are made to fit the regular Screw Bracket.

Price each $00 04
" per thousand........ .... 35 00

L. G. TILLOTSON & CO.,

Sole Agents.

Porcelain Insulator.

Porcelain Insulator for outside office use and general short line work where the regular Telegraph Insulator is not required. They are fastened to building or Cross Arm by a heavy 3-inch iron screw, are easily put up and not easily broken.

Price, with screw complete.................................... $0 05
" without screw.................................... 04

Special prices given for large quantities.

LINE WIRE.

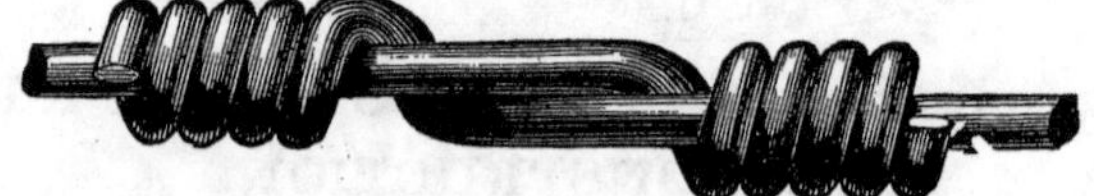

Since the introduction of JOHNSON'S WIRE into this country by us, several years ago, much greater attention has been given to the quality of line wire by telegraph companies and others constructing lines than before. Many brands of wire have been put before the public as substitutes for the superior quality manufactured by Messrs. Johnson, but the misfortune with all of them is that the proprietors do not possess the facilities for making the wire which are peculiar to Messrs. Johnson's Works. Hence the great demand for their wire in this country, resulting in sales of 16,000 miles in 1871, and 20,000 in 1872.

LINE WIRE.—Continued.

The advantages of their establishment are, in part, that their Works, covering an area of many acres, are situated directly over their own colliery, which supplies them with the coal used in smelting the pig iron. Their patent machinery, which enables them to draw their wire from the billet to a No. 8 gauge, in lengths of from 1,200 feet upwards. The advantages of great lengths must be apparent to all telegraphers. Weak spots almost invariably occur at joints. Hence the fewer joints the less breaks. Again, the process of galvanizing by this house is such, that the strength and tenacity of the wire is fully preserved instead of being impaired, as telegraph builders know, to their cost, is usually the case.

Nearly all the wires used by the English Government and Railways is purchased from Messrs. Johnson. Every particle of it is subjected to severe tests. We therefore recommend it with the utmost confidence, and point to its use by the principal telegraph companies in this country as evidence of its superiority.

The advantages of this wire over any other brand are Long Lengths, Tensile Strength, and Superior Galvanizing.

STANDARD WEIGHT AND RESISTANCE OF GALVANIZED WIRE.

	Resistance.	Weight.	Price per lb.
Weight per mile, No. 6	10 ohms	538 lbs.	
" " 7	12.1 "	461 "	
" " 8	14.1 "	389 "	
" " 9	16.4 "	323 "	
" " 10	20 "	264 "	
" " 11	25 "	211 "	
" " 12	32 7 "	163 "	
" " 14	52.8 "	97 "	
" " 16	91.6 "	57 "	

We are prepared to furnish the celebrated JOHNSON WIRE in any quantity at a moment's notice. Also the best brands of Line Wire of AMERICAN MANUFACTURE, either GALVANIZED, PLAIN, with or without galvanized joints, and BOILED IN OIL. SPECIALLY LOW PRICES GIVEN ON APPLICATION.

Componnd Copper and Steel Line Wire. Weight 160 lbs. per mile, conductivity equal to No. 8 Iron Wire.

Price per mile........ .... $40 00

OFFICE FIXTURES.

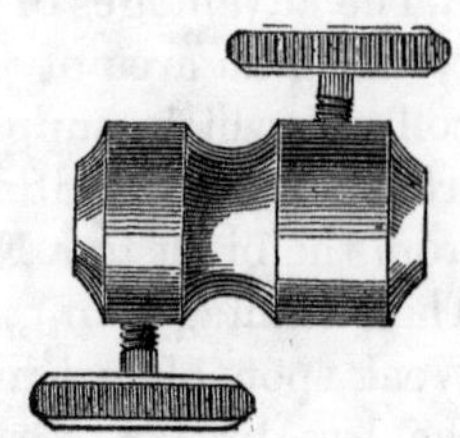

Connectors, plain, single					$0 10
" " double					15
" finished, single					15
" " double					25
Desks, Instrument Tables and Stools					
Porcelain Knobs, with Screws, per doz					50
Conducting Cord, silk,	1 conductor,	No. 1		per yard	15
" " "	1 "	No. 2		"	20
" " "	2 "	No. 3		"	20
" " "	2 "	No. 4		"	30
" " "	2 "	No. 5		"	40
" " "	2 "	No. 6		"	50

Plain Double Connector.

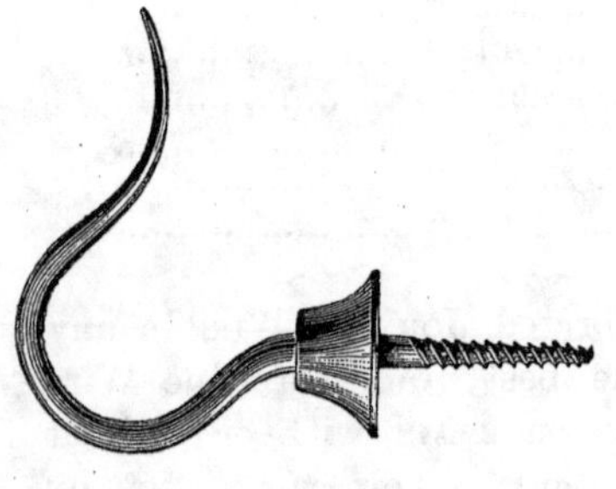

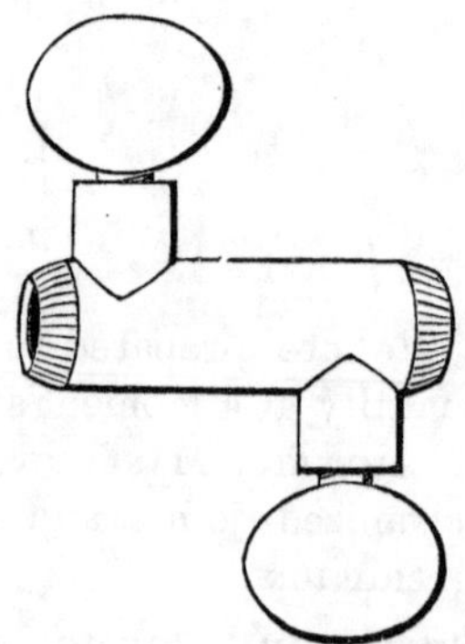

Message Hooks—per dozen, No. 1, Nickel Plated	$0 75
" " No. 1, plain	60

OFFICE WIRE BRACKETS.

FINE OAK FINISH.

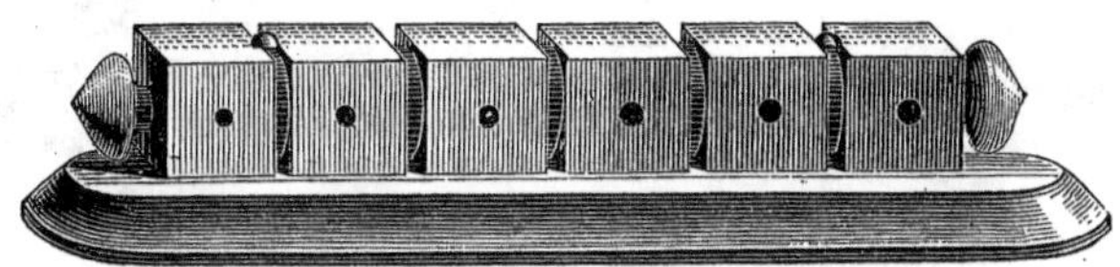

2 Holes each	$0 12
3 " "	15
4 " "	18
5 " "	20
6 " "	22
7 " "	24
8 " "	26
9 " "	28
10 " "	30
12 " "	35

Window Tubes—Heavy Glass, 3 inches each	$0 13
" " " 4 " "	15
" " " 5 " "	18
" " " 6 " "	20
" " " 8 " "	30
" " " 10 " "	38
" " " 12 " "	45
" " Hard Rubber, with heads, 2½ in	10
" " " " " 3 in	12
" " " " " 4 in	15
" " " " " 6 in	20
" " " " 16 inches long, smooth	35
" " " " 16 " " polished	50
Window Tube Binding Posts	25
Office Wire Staples, Steel, Patent Round Top, per gross	12

BUILDERS' and REPAIRERS' TOOLS.

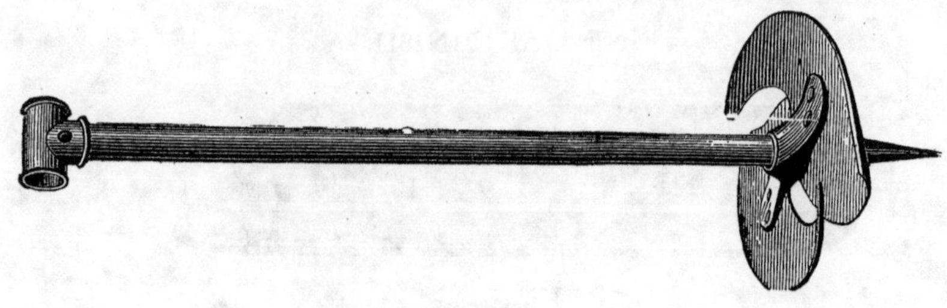

Augers—Post Hole, Patent, 10 inch	$7 00
" " " 11 inch	7 50
" " " 12 "	8 00
Bars—Digging, cast steel	3 25
" Tamping	3 00
" Tamping and Digging combined	4 25
Clamps—with Body Straps	2 50
" without Straps	1 50

Climbers—No. 1, with Straps, per pair	$3 50
" No. 2, " "	3 50
Files—All kinds at Lowest Market Price.	
File Handles—per doz.	60
Splicing Tool	75
Screw Plates—For No. 8 or 9 wire	1 00
Screw Drivers, each	25
" " extra fine, for Instruments	35 & 50
Body Belts	1 65
Tool Belts	1 50
Wire Stretchers, single	1 85
" " double	2 50
Wire Gauges, all styles	

TOOLS.—(*Continued.*)

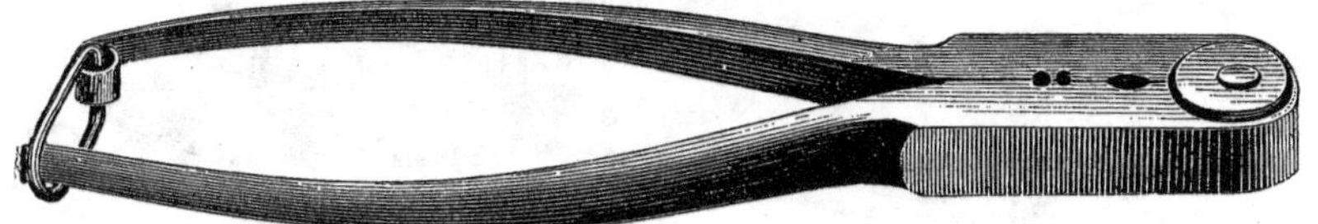

Splicing Clamps—Cast-Steel........................... $2 00

Long Gimlets—For running Office Wires, 24 inches........ 75
" " " " " " 30 " 85
" " " " " " 36 " 95
Hatchets—No. 2, 80c. No. 3.......................... 95
Hand Cars 80 00
Pulleys and Tackle—Complete......................... 2 50
Shovels—6 feet Handle. Per doz 15 00
Spoons—6 feet " " " 15 00

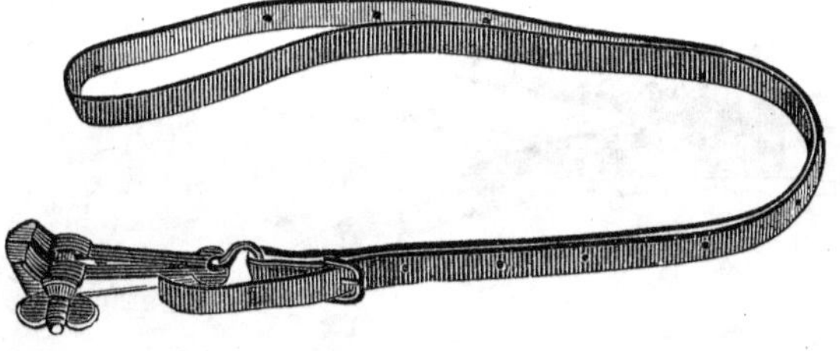

Vises—Hand .... $1 00 to 2 50
" " with Loop for Strap, Stubs.................. 2 50
Vises and Straps—Stubs.............................. 3 75
" " " —Common 2 75
Saws—Hand, $1 25, $1 75, and........................ 2 25
Tree Trimmers—Heavy................................. 3 50
Tool Bags—Leather 3 50
Line Wire Reels .... $12 00 to 15 00

PLIERS AND WIRE CUTTERS.

We make a specialty of first-class telegraph pliers, having always in stock large quantities of all the best styles of the most approved manufacturers.

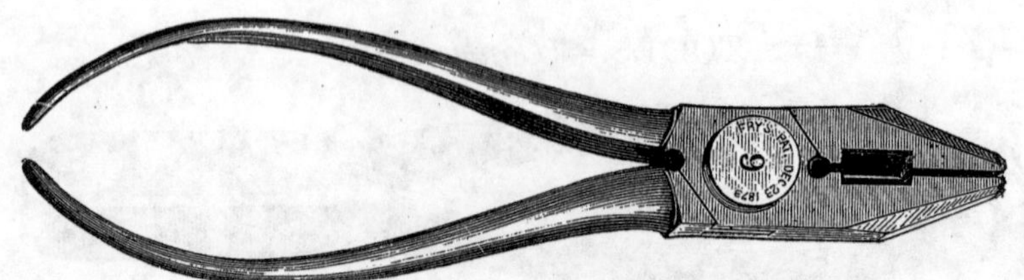

LINEMEN'S SPLICING PLIERS.

FRY'S PATENT.

[8½ inches long, with Side Cutters.]

A most convenient tool for linemen. By its use, a firm and perfect splice can be made much more easily and in less time than with common pliers. Price...$2 50

STUBS' SIDE-CUTTING PLIERS.

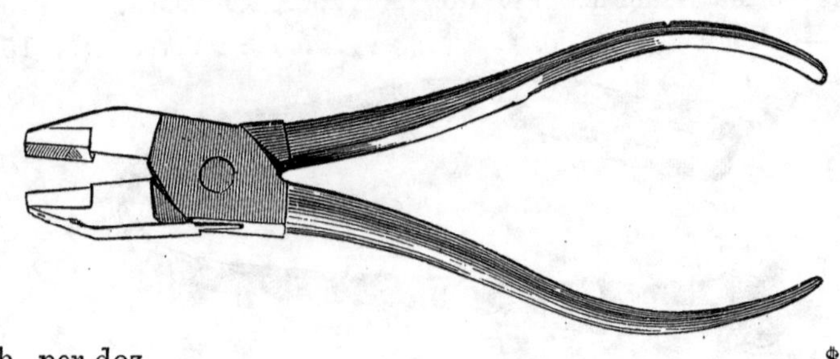

5 inch, per doz	$12 00
6 " "	15 00
7 " "	22 00
8 " "	27 00

PATENT WIRE SHEARS AND PLIERS COMBINED.

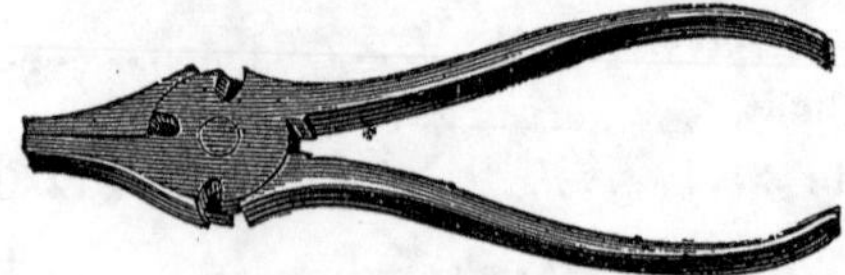

6 in., cuts anything not larger than No. 11 wire, per doz.	$12 00
8 in., " " " " No. 8 " "	15 00
10 in., " " " " No. 6 " "	20 00
5 in., French Pocket Pliers, with cutter	1 25
5 in, " " " " " nickel plated	1 50

PLAIN PLIERS.

8 inch, splicing, with holes in jaws, per doz	$12 00
8 " common, per doz	9 00
7 " " "	8 00
6 " " "	7 00

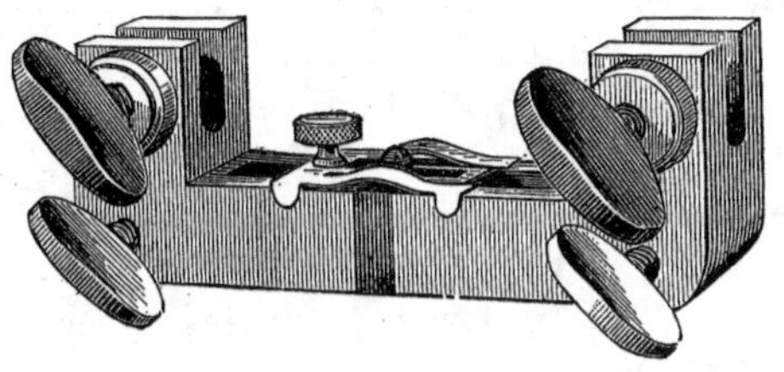

LINE TAPPING CLAMP.

For Operator's convenience in opening a wire at wrecks, or for testing, etc.

Being provided with a cut-off, it may be left in the line after using, until repairer comes along.

Price $4 50

SOLDERING APPARATUS.

Portable Alcohol Furnace, with Solder Pot		$4 50
Portable Charcoal Fire Pot		3 50
Alcohol Torches	75c. to	2 00
Blow Pipes	40c. to	75
Soldering Coppers, per pair	$1 50 to	3 00
Solder (Fine) per pound		35
" (Common) per lb.		30
Soldering Fluid, per lb.		20
Gutta Percha Bottles for Fluid, 4 oz.		60
" " " " 8 oz.		75
" " " " 16 oz.		90

STATIONERY.

Blanks and Blank Books—to order....................

Black Sheets—for Manifold, each $0 10

" " " per doz.......................... 1 00

Board Clips—No. 1, per doz............................ 7 00

" " No. 2, " 6 00

Brass " " 2 00

Enameled Sheets—for Manifold Books.................. 50

Envelopes—Plain or printed .. ..

Manifold Paper—per book, White 40

" " " Yellow........ 40

Message Paper—per lb., best............ 20

" " " common....................... 18

" " " in large quantities, special prices.

Stylus—Agate, Best Quality ....90c. and 1 00

" Steel.. 50

Sealing Wax ....

Ticket Punches—per dozen, plated 36 00

Stationery of every description to order.

BOOKS.

Chemical Physics—Pynchon................................$3 00

Cypher Letter and Telegraph Code—Larrabee........ 1 00

Electrical Tables, etc.—Clarke and Sabine.............. 5 00

Electrical Measurement—Kohlrausch 2 50

Electrical Diagrams—Davis & Rae.......................... 2 00

Electro-Metallurgy—Napier.............. .... 3 00

" " Watt.......................... 80

Electro-Magnetic Telegraph, etc.—Turnbull............ 3 00

Electro-Therapeutics—Lincoln............................ 1 50

Electricity, in Theory and Practice, 3 vols—De La Rive36 50

Electricity, its Theory, Sources, etc.—Sprague......... 3 00

Electricity and Magnetism—Jenkin 1 50

Electricity—Sir W. Snow Harris............... 60

Electricity in its relation to Practical Medicine—Meyer 4 50

Electricity and the Electric Telegraph—Prescott...... 5 00

Electricity and Magnetism—Maxwell.................10 00

Electro-Metallurgy—Gore.... .... 2 50

Electro-Therapeutics—Hamilton............................ 2 00

Examination of Telegraph Apparatus, etc.—Morse... 3 00

Frictional Electricity—Sir W. Snow Harris............ 7 00

Galvanoplastic Manipulations—Roesleuer............. 6 00

BOOKS—CONTINUED.

Galvano Therapeutics—Neftel	$1 50
Galvanism—Sir W. Snow Harris	60
Galvanometer (The) and its Uses—Haskins	1 50
Hand-Book of Practical Telegraphy—Culley	8 00
Hand-Book of English Telegraphy—Bond	1 20
Induction Coils, how made and how used—Dyer	60
History of the Telegraph—Lardner	1 75
History of Electric Telegraph—Sabine	1 20
Historical Sketch of Electric Telegraph—Jones	2 00
Lessons in Electricity—Tyndall	1 00
Manual of Telegraphy—Smith	30
Manual of Telegraphic Construction—Douglas	7 50
Manual of Electricity—Ferguson	1 75
" " —Noad	12 00
Magnetism—Noad	1 40
Magnetism—Harris	1 80
Medical Electricity—Althaus	6 00
" " —Beard & Rockwell	6 25
Modern Practice of Electric Telegraph—Pope	2 00
Natural Philosophy—Ganot	3 00
New Theory of Terrestrial Magnetism—Metcalf	2 00
Notes on Electrical Phenomena—Tyndall	75
Questions on Magnetism—McGregor	60
Reports of B. A. Committee on Electrical Standards	3 75
Telegraphy—Preece & Siveright	1 50

NICKEL PLATERS' SUPPLIES.

Chemicals, Nickel Plates, Batteries and Preparations for Polishing.

Grain Nickel	per lb...	$2 50
Pure Nickel, cast into plates	" ..	2 50
Single Sulphate of Nickel Crystals	" .	1 50
Double Sulphate of Nickel and Ammonia	" ..	1 00
Composition for Polishing	" ..	20
Rouge for finishing	per lb...75c. and	1 00

Cast Nickel Plates, $2\frac{1}{2}$x 8 inches, weigh $1\frac{3}{4}$ lbs.
" " " 4 x 7 " " $2\frac{3}{4}$ "
" " " 5 x10 " " $5\frac{1}{2}$ "
" " " 5 x12 " " $6\frac{1}{4}$ "

Special Prices made on large orders.
Prices subject to fluctuations of the market.

PROPERTIES OF COPPER WIRE.

Specific Gravity taken at 8.9.

	I.	II.	III.	IV.	V.	VI.	VII.
LINE.	BIRMINGHAM WIRE GAUGE. (*Holtzapffel.*)	DIAMETER IN MILS. (d)	AREA IN CIRCULAR MILS. (d^2)	WEIGHT. GRAINS PER FOOT.	WEIGHT. POUNDS PER 1000 FEET.	FEET PER POUND.	RESISTANCE AS PURE COPPER AT 60° IN OHMS, PER 1000 FEET.
1	1 inch square.	1000.	1273237.	26940.	3848.6	.259836	.0081251
2	1 inch round.	1000.	1000000.	21159.	3022.7	.330828	.010344
3	1 cubic inch.	325.73	106103.	2245.	320.71	3.11803	.097501
4	10	134.	17956.	379.93	54.276	18.425	.576131
5	12	109.	11881.	251.37	35.910	27.214	.870786
6	14	83.	6889.	145.76	20.823	48.023	1.50166
7	16	65.	4225.	89.397	12.771	78.30	2.4484
8	18	49.	2401.	50.803	7.258	137.79	4.3086
9	20	35.	1225.	25.920	3.703	270.06	8.6416
10	22	28.	784.	16.589	2.370	421.97	13.1951
11	23	25.	625.	13.224	1.889	529.38	16.552
12	24	22.	484.	10.241	1.463	683.53	21.3750
13	26	18.	324.	6.856	.979	1021.1	31.9290
14	28	14.	196.	4.147	.592	1687.9	52.7808
15	30	12.	144.	3.047	.435	2297.4	71.8403
16	32	9.	81.	1.714	.245	4084.2	127.715
17	34	7.	49.	1.037	.148	6751.6	211.121
18	—	**6.88**	**47.262**	**1.**	**.143**	**7000.**	**218.890**
19	35	5.	25.	.529	.076	13233.	413.780
20	36	4.	16.	.3385	.048	20677.	646.571
21	—	3.5	12.25	.2592	.037	27006.	844.49
22	—	3.	9.	.1904	.027	36759.	1149.44
23	—	**1.**	**1.**	**.021159**	**.003**	**330828.**	**10345.18**

DIMENSIONS OF WIRE GAUGE SIZES IN DECIMAL PARTS OF AN INCH.

No of Wire Gauge.	Size of each No. in decimal parts of an inch of the American Wire Gauge.	Size of each No. in decimal parts of an inch of the Birmingham Wire Gauge.	No. of Wire Gauge.	Size of each No. in decimal parts of an inch of the American Wire Gauge.	Size of each No. in decimal parts of an inch of the Birmingham Wire Gauge.
0000	.460	.454	19	.03539	.042
000	.40964	.425	20	.03196	.035
00	.36480	.380	21	.02846	.032
0	.32495	.340	22	.02535	.028
1	.28930	.300	23	.02257	.025
2	.25763	.284	24	.0201	.022
3	.22942	.259	25	.0179	.020
4	.20431	.238	26	.01594	.018
5	.18194	.220	27	.01419	.016
6	.16202	.203	28	.01264	.014
7	.14428	.180	29	.01126	.013
8	.12849	.165	30	.01002	.012
9	.11443	.148	31	.00893	.010
10	.10189	.134	32	.00795	.009
11	.09074	.120	33	.00708	.008
12	.08081	.109	34	.0063	.007
13	.07196	.095	35	.00561	.005
14	.06408	.083	36	.005	.004
15	.05707	.072	37	.00445	
16	.05082	.065	38	.00396	
17	.04525	.058	39	.00353	
18	.0403	.049	40	.00314	

DECIMALS EQUALING PARTS OF AN INCH.

$\frac{1}{64}$ = .0156	$\frac{11}{64}$ = .1718
$\frac{1}{32}$ = .0312	$\frac{3}{16}$ = .1875
$\frac{3}{64}$ = .0468	$\frac{13}{64}$ = .2031
$\frac{1}{16}$ = .0625	$\frac{7}{32}$ = .2187
$\frac{5}{64}$ = .0781	$\frac{15}{64}$ = .2343
$\frac{3}{32}$ = .0937	$\frac{1}{4}$ = .2500
$\frac{7}{64}$ = .1093	$\frac{17}{64}$ = .2656
$\frac{1}{8}$ = .1250	$\frac{9}{32}$ = .2812
$\frac{9}{64}$ = .1406	$\frac{19}{64}$ = .2968
$\frac{5}{32}$ = .1562	$\frac{5}{16}$ = .3125

In the table on page 108, lines 1, 2 and 3 are given chiefly as data of calculation. Line 3 is one cubic inch of copper converted into a foot length. The weights, column 5, and the resistances, column 7, are given for 1,000 feet for convenience of calculation on the decimal system. When multiplied by 5.28 they give the figures for one mile. Almost any information required may be found from the data given in this table by very simple calculations. For example, if we wish to learn the resistance of a pound weight of any size, it can be ascertained by dividing the number in column 7 by that in column 5.

Line 18 is the wire, of which one foot in length weighs one grain, which forms the basis of calculation. Line 23 is a wire of One Mil. or .001 in diameter. These two lines, therefore, furnish constants applicable to calculations of every description.

INSULATED WIRES.

Please observe that all of our Office and Magnet wires are drawn by the *American Gauge*, and consequently there is a greater number of feet in a pound of our No. 14 than in a pound of No. 14 by the Birmingham Gauge, by which wire is generally drawn. Our No. 12 corresponds with No. 14, and our No. 14 with No. 16, Birmingham Gauge. Buyers will do well to bear this in mind, as we believe our list of Office and Magnet wires is the only one giving prices by American Gauge.

[By reference to the above table, the difference between American and Birmingham Gauge can easily be ascertained.]

OFFICE WIRES.

No. 12, Gutta Percha, Covered, per pound	$1 40
" 14, " " " " "	1 60
" 16, " " " " "	1 75
" 18, " " " " "	2 00

BISHOP'S NEW COMPOUND FOR OFFICE AND OUT-DOOR USE.

No. 12, per foot	05
" 14, "	04
" 16, "	03½
" 18, "	02½

KERITE COVERED WIRE (STUBS' GAUGE.)

No. 14, Single Covered, per foot	06
" 14, Double " "	07
" 16, Single " "	05
" 16, Double " "	06
" 18, Single " "	04
Kerite Sheet, for wrapping splices in office wires, per lb.	2 00
" Tape, per roll	2 00

RED AND WHITE BRAIDED, PARAFFINED AND COMPRESSED COTTON AND LINEN DOUBLE COVERED OFFICE WIRES.

No. 12, 45 feet per pound, per pound	75
" 14, 66 " " "	75
" 16, 83 " " "	75
" 18, 132 " " "	75
" 20, 170 " " "	1 00

These wires in any other colors at the same prices.

PATENT BRAIDED WATERPROOF POLISHED OFFICE WIRES.

No. 12, per pound	80
" 14, "	80
" 16, "	80
" 18, "	80

BURGLAR ALARM, CALL BELL AND ANNUNCIATOR WIRES.

Double Cotton Wrapped, Waxed and Paraffined.

No. 18, 155 feet per pound, per pound	70
" 19, 200 " " "	70
" 20, 239 " " "	70

GUTTA PERCHA COVERED WIRES.

AMERICAN GAUGE.

FOR SUBMARINE USE.

No.	Description.	Outside Gauge.	Feet per lb.	Price per foot.	Pounds per mile.	Price per lb.
8	2 Coats Gutta Percha.......	1	13	20c.	413	$2 00
10	2 " "	2	20	13	267	2 25
12	2 " "	5	34	08	154	2 50
14	2 " "	5	41	08	123	2 75
14	2 " "	2	30	10	176	2 75
14	2 " "	0	24	15	216	2 75

FOR OFFICE AND ELECTRIC USES.

No.	Description.	Outside Gauge.	Feet per lb.	Price by foot.	Pounds per mile.	Price per lb.
14	1 Coat Gutta Percha........	7	51	04c.	104 lbs.	$1 60
15						1 65
16	1 " "	8	72	03½	73 "	1 75
17						1 85
18	1 " "	9	126	02½	42 "	2 00
19						2 10
20	1 " "	11	176	02	30 "	2 25
21						2 35
22	1 " "	11	230	01½	23 "	2 50
23						2 75
24	1 " "	13	330	01½	16 "	3 00
25						3 25
26	1 " "	14	480	01	11 "	3 50
27						3 75
28	1 " "	15	586	¾	9 "	4 00
29						4 25
30						4 50
31	1 " "	17	1240	0½	4¼ "	4 75

FOR BLASTING PURPOSES.

No.	Description.	Outside Gauge.	Feet per lb.	Price per foot.	Pounds per mile.	Price per lb.
24	Cop. 2 Conductor's.........	7	100	03½	48 to mile,	$3 50
18	" 2 "	2	32	10	161 "	3 00
19	Iron 1 "	11	132	02	35 "	2 25

MISCELLANEOUS INSULATED WIRES.

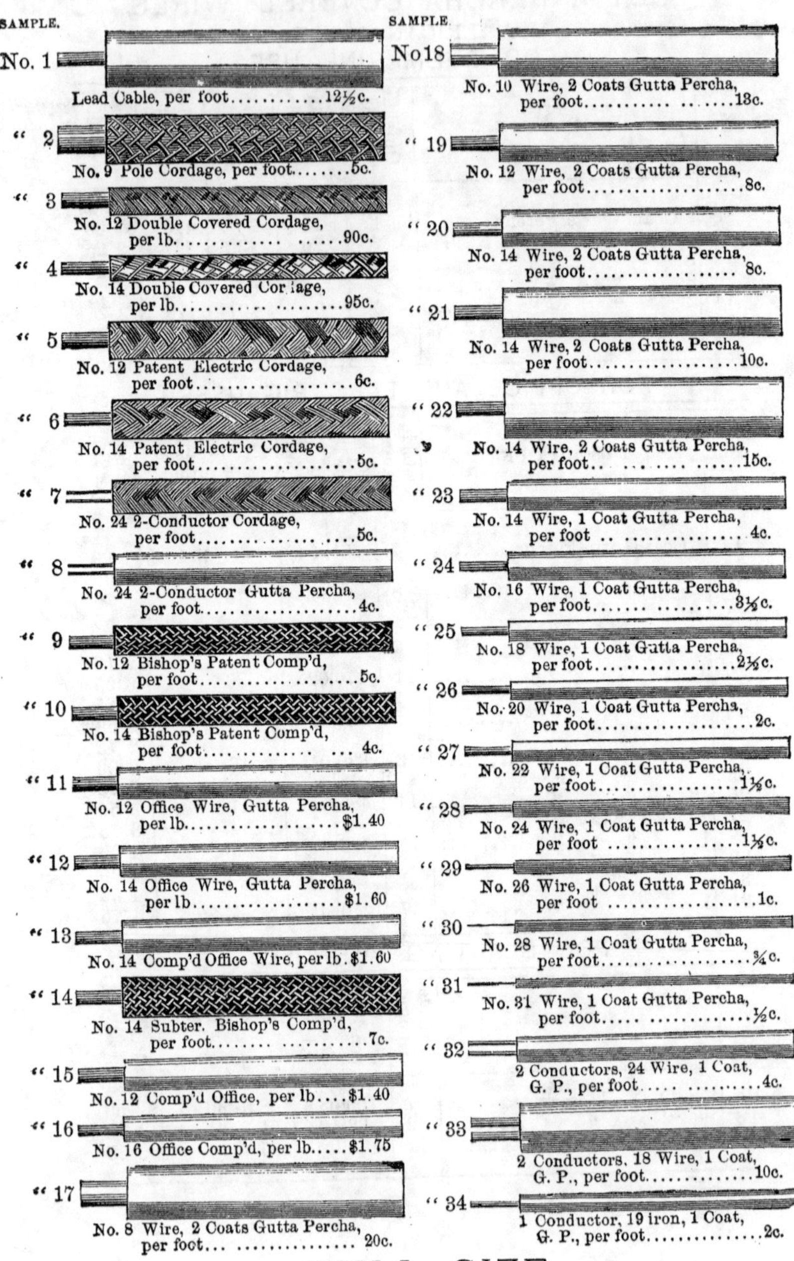

SAMPLE.

No. 1 Lead Cable, per foot............12½c.

" 2 No. 9 Pole Cordage, per foot........5c.

" 3 No. 12 Double Covered Cordage, per lb.............. ......90c.

" 4 No. 14 Double Covered Cordage, per lb............ ....95c.

" 5 No. 12 Patent Electric Cordage, per foot.....................6c.

" 6 No. 14 Patent Electric Cordage, per foot.....................5c.

" 7 No. 24 2-Conductor Cordage, per foot.....................5c.

" 8 No. 24 2-Conductor Gutta Percha, per foot.....................4c.

" 9 No. 12 Bishop's Patent Comp'd, per foot.....................5c.

" 10 No. 14 Bishop's Patent Comp'd, per foot............... ... 4c.

" 11 No. 12 Office Wire, Gutta Percha, per lb.....................$1.40

" 12 No. 14 Office Wire, Gutta Percha, per lb.....................$1.60

" 13 No. 14 Comp'd Office Wire, per lb. $1.60

" 14 No. 14 Subter. Bishop's Comp'd, per foot........ ....7c.

" 15 No. 12 Comp'd Office, per lb....$1.40

" 16 No. 16 Office Comp'd, per lb.....$1.75

" 17 No. 8 Wire, 2 Coats Gutta Percha, per foot... .... 20c.

SAMPLE.

No18 No. 10 Wire, 2 Coats Gutta Percha, per foot.......... ....18c.

" 19 No. 12 Wire, 2 Coats Gutta Percha, per foot.....................8c.

" 20 No. 14 Wire, 2 Coats Gutta Percha, per foot..................... 8c.

" 21 No. 14 Wire, 2 Coats Gutta Percha, per foot.....................10c.

" 22 No. 14 Wire, 2 Coats Gutta Percha, per foot.. ....15c.

" 23 No. 14 Wire, 1 Coat Gutta Percha, per foot .. ..4c.

" 24 No. 16 Wire, 1 Coat Gutta Percha, per foot....... ....3½c.

" 25 No. 18 Wire, 1 Coat Gutta Percha, per foot.................2½c.

" 26 No. 20 Wire, 1 Coat Gutta Percha, per foot.....................2c.

" 27 No. 22 Wire, 1 Coat Gutta Percha, per foot.................1½c.

" 28 No. 24 Wire, 1 Coat Gutta Percha, per foot ....1½c.

" 29 No. 26 Wire, 1 Coat Gutta Percha, per foot ....1c.

" 30 No. 28 Wire, 1 Coat Gutta Percha, per foot.....................¾c.

" 31 No. 31 Wire, 1 Coat Gutta Percha, per foot..... ....½c.

" 32 2 Conductors, 24 Wire, 1 Coat, G. P., per foot..... ....4c.

" 33 2 Conductors, 18 Wire, 1 Coat, G. P., per foot.............10c.

" 34 1 Conductor, 19 iron, 1 Coat, G. P., per foot...............2c.

FULL SIZE.

MAGNET WIRES.

Our silk-covered and cotton-covered Magnet Wires are of *extraordinary* quality in the following respects, *purity* and *high conductivity of the copper wire* used, all of which is carefully tested and selected before covering.

Fine and *perfectly regular covering*, by which we get the highest insulation that can be obtained with silk or cotton winding in the *smallest outward diameter yet attained.*

Our machines for this purpose are entirely new and unlike any others yet adopted, and the results produced in the extraordinary quality of magnet wires turned out are as near perfection as can be desired.

The great importance of a perfectly regular covering, which is of the least possible thickness, and at the same time an absolute insulation, cannot be too highly estimated.

SIZE, NO.	COTTON COVERED.		SILK COVERED.	
	FEET PER POUND.	PRICE.	FEET PER POUND.	PRICE.
8	18	$0 50		
9		50		
10	27	52		
11		52		
12	51	52		
13		54		
14	83	54		
15		54		
16	110	60		$1 60
17		60		1 75
18	176	65		1 75
19	252	65		1 85
20	352	70	310	1 85
21	450	75	470	1 95
22		80		1 95
23		90		2 20
24	640	1 00	796	2 20
25		1 20	1088	2 40
26	1056	1 20		2 40
27		1 40		2 75
28	1625	1 40	1920	2 75
29		1 65		3 40
30		1 65	2336	3 40
31	1840	1 90		3 80
32	2112	1 90	2912	4 00
34				4 75
35				6 00
36				8 00
38				14 00

The above prices are for quantities of *one lb. and upward.* We will sell the fine sizes *by the ounce at* 20 *per cent.*, and by quarter and half pounds at 10 *per cent. advance* on pound prices.

No. 36, Silk-covered on Spools............ 1 oz. 75c. 2 oz. $1 50
No. 38 " " " .... 1 " $1 00 2 " 2 00

ELECTRO-MEDICAL APPARATUS.

HALL'S NEW PATENT

Three-Current French Battery.

Consisting of Battery and Helix, Connecting Wires, Sponge Handles, two silver-plated Handles and Insulators, box of bichromate of potash and extra zinc, so that a person having one of these Batteries can travel with it and have all the materials necessary to operate it for six months.

This Instrument is entirely different from any other Battery. It produces three distinct currents, and can be regulated either by the Regulating Rod, or by the immersion of the zinc in the solution. It can be so controlled as to obtain the finest or strongest electrical sensation.

The Armature vibrates on an elastic substance, thus regulating the vibrations and producing one continuous and thrilling current of Electricity.

Great pains have been taken in their manufacture, thus rendering them not liable to become out of order. In fact, from their thorough construction, no portion can get out of repair except the zinc; this will, of course, wear out, but will last twelve months, with every-day use, and can be replaced at a cost of twenty-five cents.

Apparatus, complete....................................	$15 00
Extra Battery, per cell, complete..........................	3 00
Extra Zincs, amalgamated............................	25

Liberal Discount to the Trade.

Dr. JEROME KIDDER'S

Celebrated Electro-Medical Apparatus,

All Styles at Manufacturers' Prices.

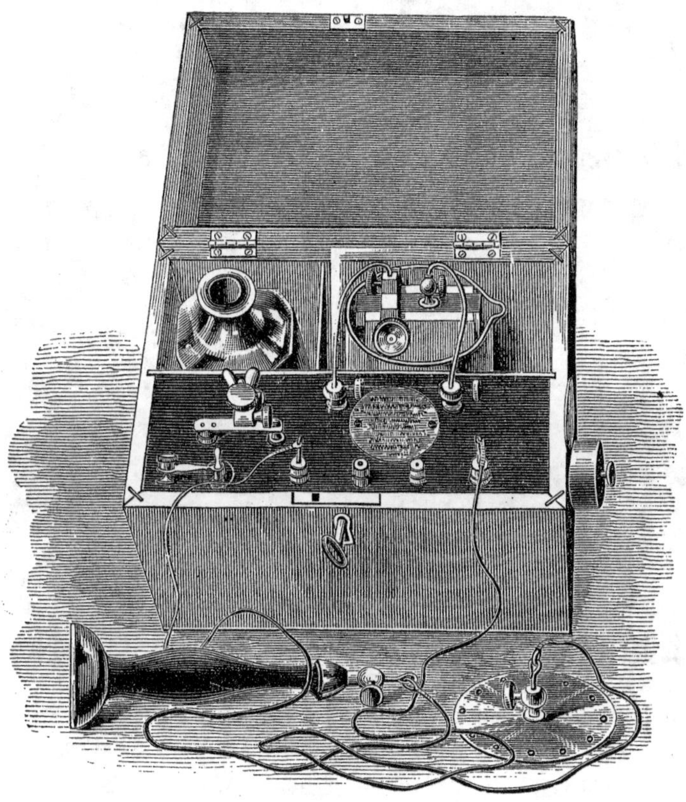

No. 4.

Office and Family Machine.

No. 4 has three coils and six variations of the qualities of the currents, and is operated by one open battery, which is for weeks and months constantly ready for use, without changing the fluid, and a bottle accompanies, into which the fluid can be poured whenever desired. Price, $20.00

The Apparatuses, No. 4 and No. 5 are most in demand. Though presenting a good appearance, they are not made for show. The coils of all the genuine Dr. Kidder's machines are constructed with reference to the medical qualities of electricity, without regard to expense.

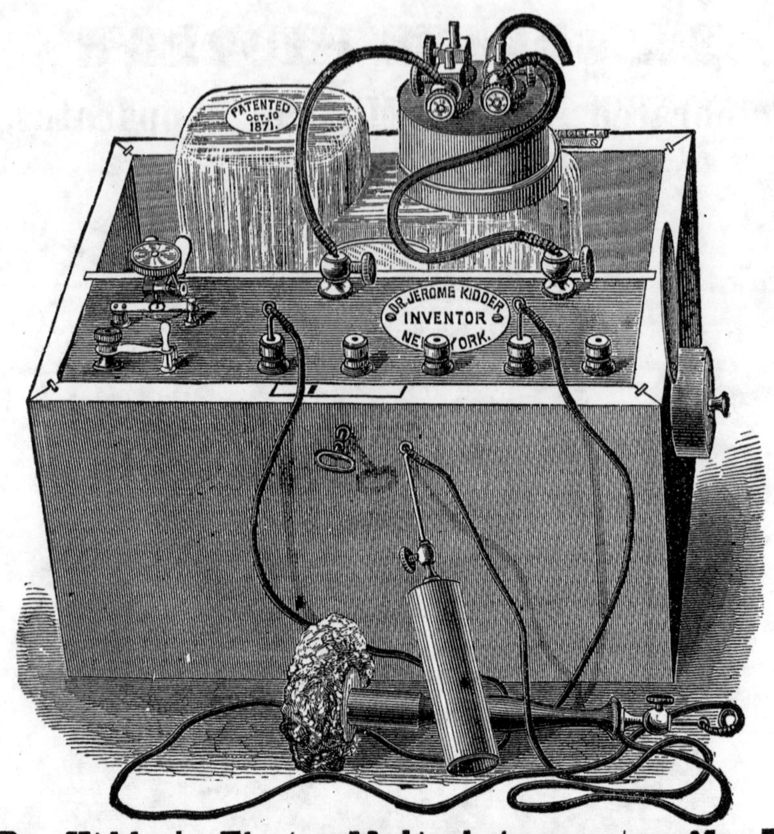

Dr. Kidder's Electro-Medical Apparatus No. 5,

With *four differently conditioned coils,* each arranged to use in various combinations, producing *ten different qualities of electricity.*

Price, with Hydrostat Tip Battery, $27.00. With Open Battery, $24.00

SMALL ELECTRO-MEDICAL MACHINES

For Family use, similar to No. 4.

THREE CURRENTS...........$15.00. SIX CURRENTS..... ....$18.00

These are first-class machines, but because of the superior merits as to the qualities of the currents of the No. 4 and No. 5 machines, Dr. Kidder recommends these in preference.

Tip Battery, per cell.......................... ....$6 50

Open Silver-plate Smee Battery, per cell..................... 3 00

ALL APPLIANCES and MATERIALS for KIDDER APPARATUS and BATTERIES at MANUFACTURERS' PRICES.

ELECTRO-MEDICAL APPARATUS.

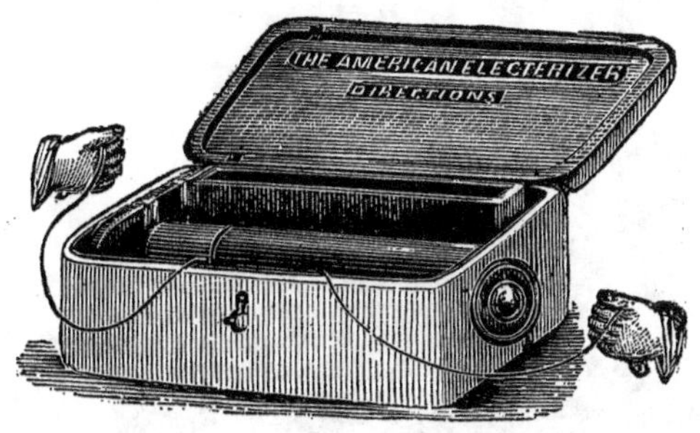

POCKET MEDICAL INSTRUMENT, with Conducting Cords and Handles complete, very powerful $6 00

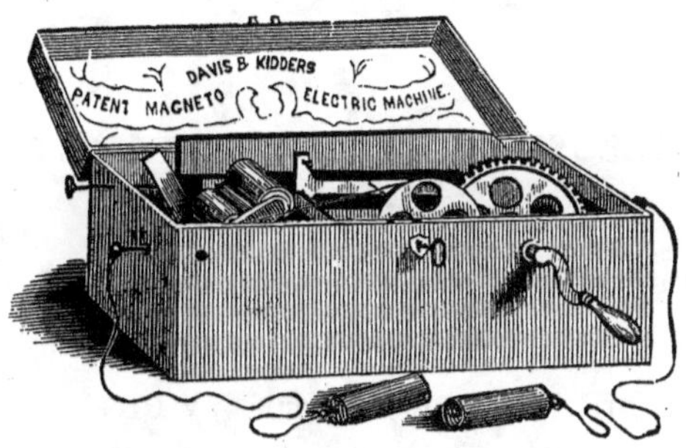

MAGNETO-ELECTRIC MACHINES.

Complete, in fine finished Case $10 00

We sell every style of Electro-Medical Apparatus in the market at manufacturers' prices, and manufacture to order any special apparatus that may be required for the Application of Electricity.

We will also purchase for our Customers any Goods they may desire, whether in our line or not, and ship them at the lowest market price.

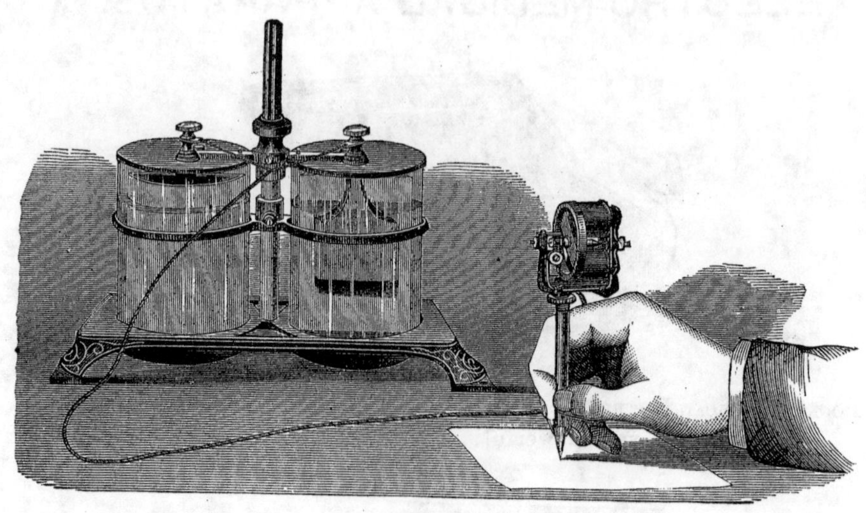

THE EDISON ELECTRIC PEN AND DUPLICATING PRESS.

For making any number of Fac-simile Copies of Letters, Orders, Circulars, Diagrams, etc. No skill required for its operation, which is as simple as that of an ordinary Letter Copy Press.

Price, complete outfit, with Battery ready for work :

No. 1, with Press, 7x11 inches	....	$40 00
" 2 " " 9x11 "	....	45 00
" 3 " " 9x14 "	....	50 00

The Double Cell Battery, mounted in ornamental stand, for running Electric Pen, Medical Instruments, small Electric Motors, Laboratory purposes, etc., may be had separate.

Price, complete $6 50

INDUCTION COILS.

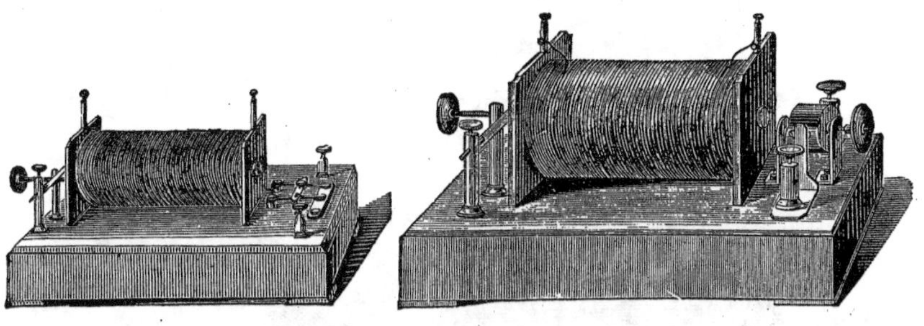

Coil, with Automatic Break, Spark of 1-16th inch	$7 50
" " " " " 1/8 inch	10 00
" " " " " 1/4 "	15 00
Similar Coil, with Spark of 1/2 inch	22 00
" " " " 3/4 "	38 00
" " " " 1 "	45 00
" " " " 1 1/4 to 1 1/2 inch	60 00
" " " Commutator, with Spark of 2 inches	100 00
" " " " " " 3 "	140 00

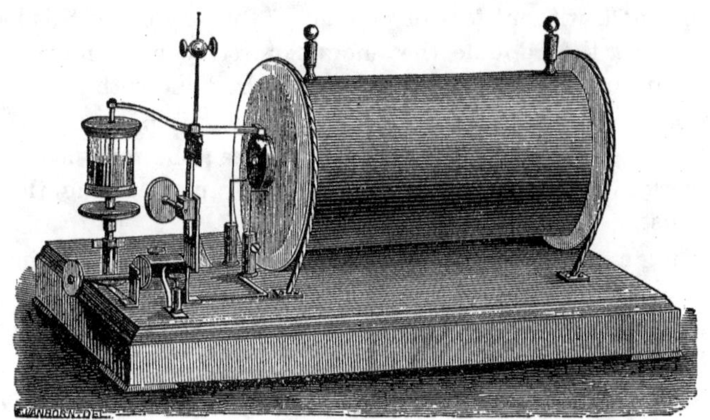

Coil, with Foucault's Automatic Break and Commutator, Spark of 4 inches	$225 00
Coil, with very highest style of finish, with Commutator and Foucalt's *Double Mercurial* Contact Breaker on *separate stand,* Spark of 9 inches and over	400 00

Electric Apparatus for Blasting.

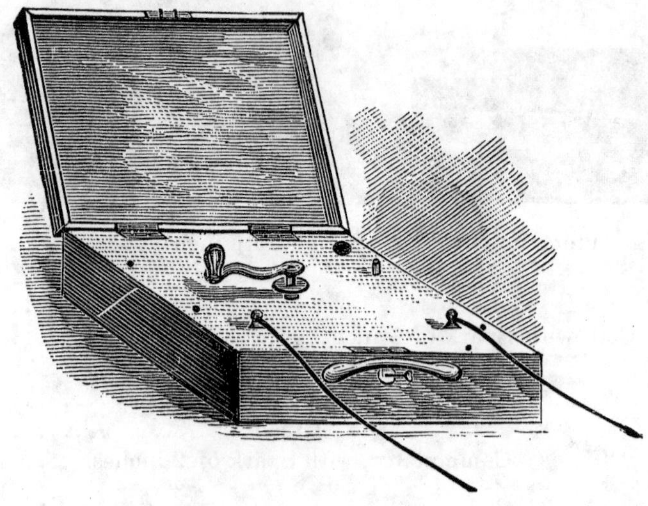

It is claimed, without fear of challenge, that by using this battery with skill, *more* than double the amount of *rock* can be moved with a given amount of material than can possibly be done with safety fuse.

It is much more reliable than safety fuse ; it is perfectly safe ; no accident *can possibly* happen from hanging fire ; the men need not be off the work more than a few seconds ; it is rapidly taking the place of safety fuse.

By firing a number of charges at the same instant of time, the whole *power* of the explosive material is utilized and at once brought into action, which far exceeds the same amount of material in *force* of single charges fired in rotation.

For economy and safety, nothing of the kind in modern science is equal to it, and it is *all* we claim for it. The battery will give a spark of more than 2½ inches in length, and may be used for any purpose where an electric spark is required ; it is always reliable, as it is not affected by atmospheric changes. The whole apparatus is contained in a black walnut case 6x14x14 inches, supplied with handles whereby it can be easily carried about. Full directions for use sent out with each battery.

ELECTRIC APPARATUS FOR BLASTING.

PRICES.

Friction Electric Battery	$75 00
Magneto " "	25 00
Battery fuses, 4 feet length	05
" 6 "	06
" 8 "	10
Detached fuses	04
Leading Wire, per foot	04
Connecting Wire, per lb	70

Dualin Fuses, each 2 cents extra.

Fuses with gutta percha insulation, per foot 1 cent extra.

Fuses of any required length of wire to order.

Special prices given for large quantities.

In ordering fuses please say whether they are for FRICTION or MAGNETO Battery.

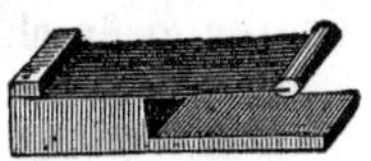

THE "SNAPPER" SOUNDER (PATENTED.)

Snapper Sounder, plain, with Book	$0 25
" " " " " ½ doz	1 20
" " " " " per doz	1 75
" " nickel plated, with Book, each	50
" " with Rubber Knob	75
" " Frog Pattern, without Book, each	20
" " per dozen	1 25

EXTRACTS

From Letters received from a few of our Customers.

"Your beautiful instruments compare favorably with the best Morse apparatus in Europe." S. F. B. Morse.

"Substantial in make and tasteful in design."
W. J. Holmes, *Supt.*

"Superior to any we have in use." E. A. Calahan, *Supt.*

"Have given entire satisfaction, and cannot be excelled."
W. S. Putnam, *Supt.*

"Toughest wire I ever handled. Instruments have given entire satisfaction." H. W. Stager, *Supt.*

"I have never seen any work surpassing yours."
J. Desmond, *Supt.*

Not a single instance of imperfection has come to my notice."
M. L. Wood, *Supt.*

"Reliable in every respect." Chas. Petersen, *Supt.*

"Your work has given every satisfaction."
W. H. Heiss, *Supt.*

"Workmanship and finish is all that can be desired."
T. H. Miles, *Supt.*

"I beg to express my satisfaction with the work I have had from your firm, and the manner in which my orders have been executed."
J. M. Nye, *Supt.*

"Permit me to express my entire satisfaction with your Instruments, which I have been using for the past three years."
A. G. Davis, *Supt.*

"Your Instruments are the best in finish and workmanship I have ever seen, and work splendidly."
A. B. Spooner, *Division Operator.*

"I have always found your Instruments to give good satisfaction, and can fully endorse them as first-class in every respect."

G. Bogert, *Supt.*

"I have been using Instruments of your manufacture, and find them superior to those of any others in use on our lines, of which there are many patterns."

F. G. Moffett, *Chief Operator.*

"The Combination Instrument is the best thing of the kind I have ever seen, and is all you claim for it."

C. S. Jones, *Manager.*

"I have tried your Combination Instrument in a circuit of 660 miles, and it gives perfect satisfaction."

F. M. Speed, *Supt.*

"The Relays, Keys, and Sounders purchased of you from time to time have given entire satisfaction." G. R. Brown, *Supt.*

"I deem it due to you to say that, in my judgment, you have given the Telegraph the best instruments manufactured."

J. L. Mingle, *Supt.*

"The Johnson Wire is splendid — not a break in the whole cable." S. C. Bishop.

We have many others of similar import from parties who do not wish publicity given to their expressions of preference.

MANUFACTURERS AND DEALERS

IN

Telegraph Materials

OF EVERY DESCRIPTION.

GEISSLER'S VACUA TUBES.

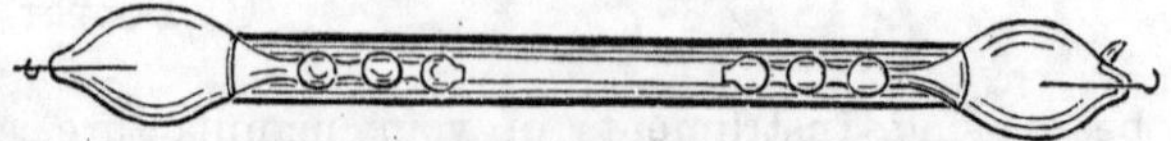

It would be quite impossible, by any description, to do justice to the extreme beauty of the phenomena observed when the inductive discharge is passed through many of the tubes so ingeniously prepared by M Geissler; and when these tubes are so arranged that continuous rotary motion can be given to them very beautiful effects are produced. By causing them to rotate with different degrees of velocity, and altering the frequency of the discharge and direction of the current, various optical phenomena are brought out, which greatly increase the magnificence of the display.

Plain or Spiral Tubes in great variety, six inches long		$0 80
Same, with bulbs or tube of Uranium Glass	$1 00 to	1 30
Tubes with Uranium Glass, 7 to 8 ins. long, finely finished		1 60
Tubes of various styles, with Uranium Glass Bulb, Spirals		2 50
Fluorescent Double Tube, 8 to 9 inches long		3 60
Double Tube, 15 "		5 50
" " 19 "		6 50
" " 24 "		7 50
" " 30 "		10 00
U-Tubes, 9 inches long		6 00
Spectrum Tubes, every variety, each		3 00
Tubes 12 inches high, containing either a Cross or a Vase of Uranium Glass		6 50
Tubes 18 inches long, with large bulbs for showing *stratification* of the electric light		5 50

Various Tubes, single, double and U-shape, filled with fluorescent Solutions, Phosphorescent Solids, &c., from $2.60 to $7.00 each.

ROTATORS,

OR SMALL ELECTRICAL ENGINES FOR ROTATING GEISSLER'S TUBES.

No. 1, for 6 to 8 inch Tubes	$10 50
" 2, " 10 to 20 " "	25 00

[We put up small experimental sets of these tubes with Battery, Rotator and Coil to operate them, packed ready for Shipping, at $35.00.]

Geissler Tube, $6.50.

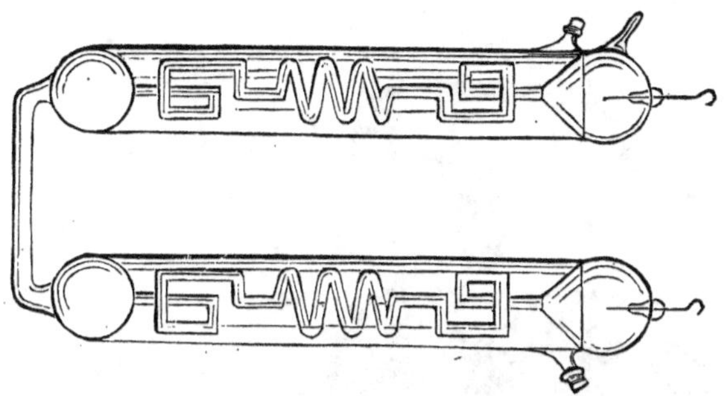

Cuban Pattern.
Insulator, 30c.

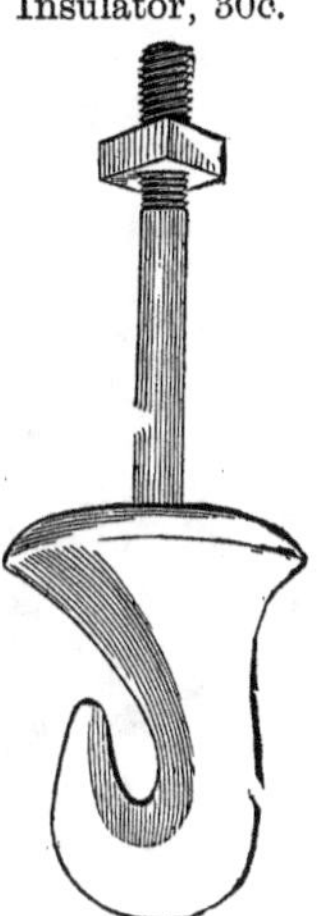

No. 1, Box Bell, $2.50.

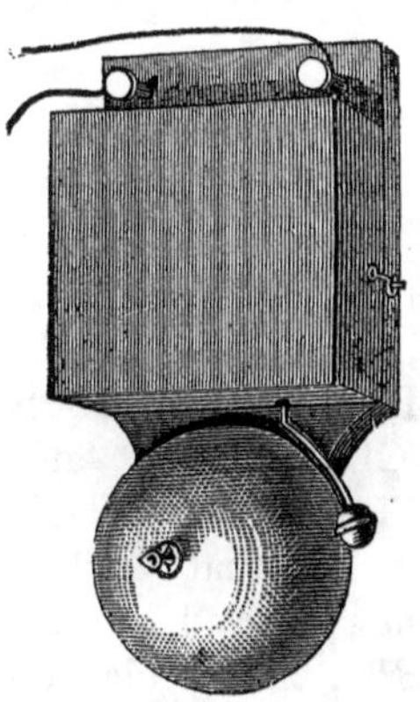

Rubber Hook Insulator, 17c.

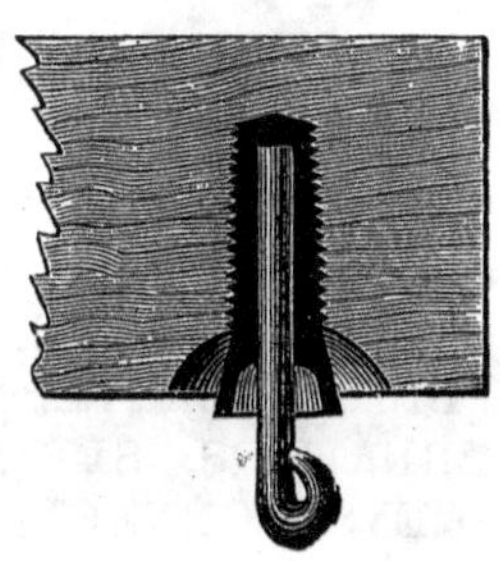

Register Reel, $3.00

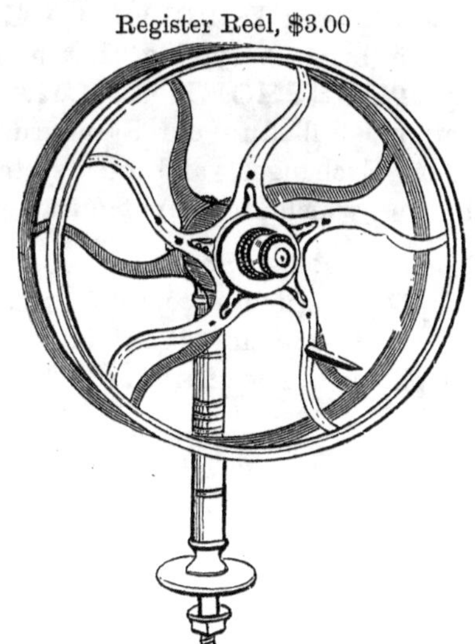

Register Weight and Pulley, $1.75.

Telephone Materials.

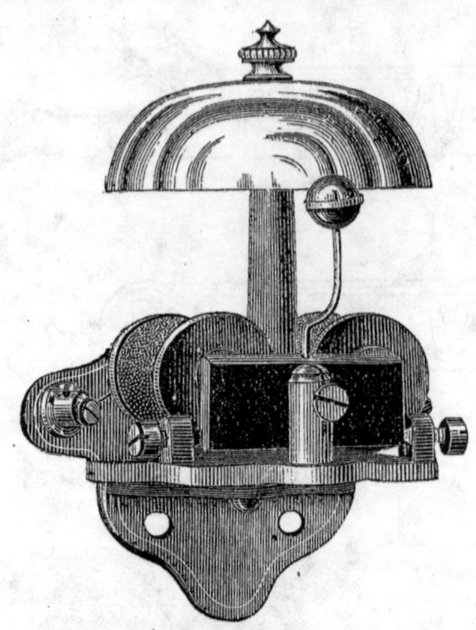

(STANDARD TELEPHONE BELL.)

We manufacture and keep on hand all kinds of TELEPHONE MATERIALS, such as SWITCHES, CUT OUTS, COMMUTATORS, MAGNETO CALL BELLS, BATTERY CALL BELLS, CROSS BARS, CIRCUIT BREAKERS, SPRING JACKS, OPEN and CLOSED CIRCUIT KEYS, CONNECTING PINS and WEDGES, SINGLE and DOUBLE CONNECTING CORDS in great variety, and in brief everything that is required to construct and operate any **TELEPHONE EXCHANGE SYSTEM.** Particular attention is called to our Standard Telephone Bell (see cut) for Telephone Exchanges, and our system of Switches for Telephone Exchanges, which are simple, durable and perfect in their operation.

Telephone Bells, (Standard) $3 00
Telephone Switches complete, with Bells, Spring Jacks, Cords and Connecting Pins .... $5 50 to 8 00

Telephone	Connecting	Cords,	Worsted	Covered,	Single,	No. 1.	15c.
"	"	"	"	"	Double	" 1.	30c.
"	"	"	"	"	Single	" 2.	15c.
"	"	"	"	"	Double	" 2.	35c.
"	"	"	"	"	Single	" 3.	14c.
"	"	"	"	"	Double	" 3.	30c.

Telephone appliances made to order to meet any requirements.

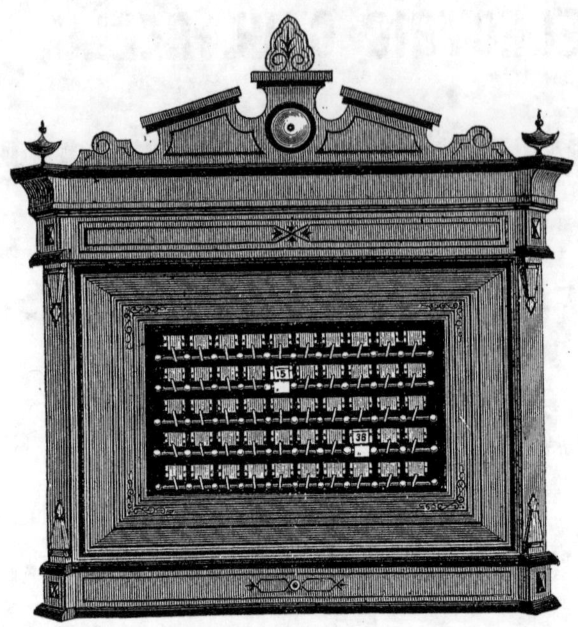

Improved Electrical Annunciators

of the best construction and most elegant design, adapted for reliable operation *without repairs*, for years.

First Premium American Institute (Report of the Judges) : "We consider this Hotel and House Annunciator equal in its operation and superior in its mode of construction and arrangement to any other."

Style No. 1 (Nickel-plated drops),	for 4 Rooms	....	$26 00
" " 1 " "	" 6 "	....	30 00
" " 1 " "	" 8 "	....	35 00
" " 1 " "	" 10 "	....	42 00
" " 1, over 10 drops, $3.50 for each additional drop.			

Special Prices made on large Annunciators, and estimates for putting them up furnished upon application.

Liberal Discounts to Agents and the Trade.

IMPROVED ELECTRICAL ANNUNCIATORS.

Style No. 3, mounted in cases similar to No. 1, only in place of the nickel plated drops outside of the face, the drops are inside, and the face is furnished with transparent spaces, through which the numbers are shown when the drops fall.

No. 3 Annunciator, for	4 Rooms	....	$16 00
" 3 "	" 6 "	....	18 00
" 3 "	" 8 "	....	22 00
" 3 "	" 10 "	....	26 00

Over 10 rooms, $2.00 for each additional drop.

Specially low prices made on large Annunciators.

☞ LIBERAL DISCOUNTS TO AGENTS AND THE TRADE.

Improved Automatic Burglar Alarm.

The most reliable, the best finished, and finest working Burglar Alarm ever offered to the public.

Extract from Report of the Judges of the American Institute:

"We consider this Electric Burglar Alarm as *first in the order of Merit*, for the *perfection and simplicity with which, in its construction*, its various workings are performed, and the *highest quality of workmanship*. We would most respectfully recommend the award of a SILVER MEDAL."

IMPROVED

AUTOMATIC BURGLAR ALARM.

PRICES.

No. 1 Style, for	4 Rooms			$32 00
" 1 "	"	6	"	36 00
" 1 "	"	8	"	40 00
" 1 "	"	10	"	50 00
" 1 "	"	12	"	60 00
" 3 "	"	4	"	20 00
" 3 "	"	6	"	22 00
" 3 "	"	8	"	28 00
" 3 "	"	10	"	32 00
" 3 "	"	12	"	36 00

BATTERIES

FOR

ANNUNCIATORS & BURGLAR ALARMS.

We have adopted the celebrated Leclanché Battery for all Burglar Alarm and House Bells, as it contains no acids or poisonous substances, has no odor, and *we guarantee them to work one year* (they have been in some houses over three [3] years), *without any attention* from the owner.

The Battery is in a neat box, as in the above cut, and may be placed anywhere in the house.

4 Cells, Sealed Battery, in box $12 00

ELECTRIC BELLS.

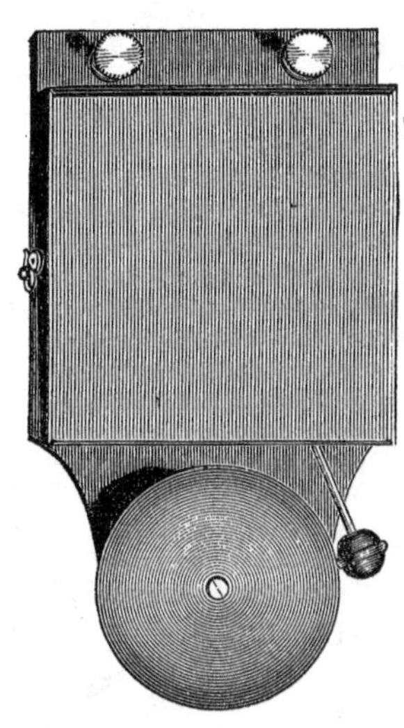

BOX BELL.

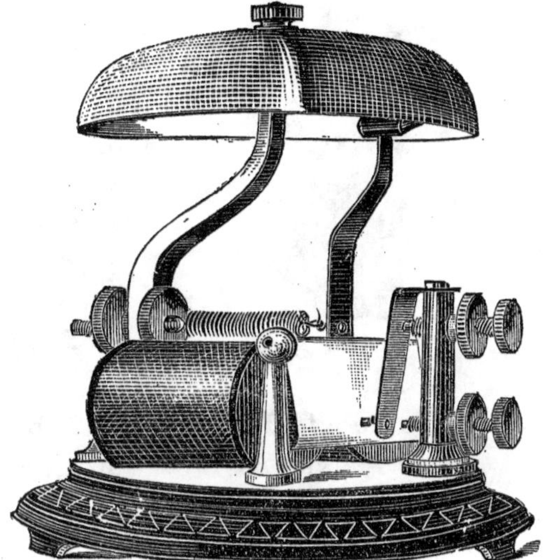

CIRCULAR BASE TABLE BELL.

Box Bell, in finely polished Mahogany Cases.

No. 1, with 2½ inch bell	$2 50
" 2, " 3½ " "	3 00
" 3, " 4 " "	4 00
" 4, " 5 " "	6 00
" 5, " 6 " "	7 00

Circular Base Table or Bracket Bells, finely finished.

No. 1, with 3 inch bell	$5 50
" 2, " 3½ " "	6 00
" 3, " 4 " "	6 50

ELECTRIC BELLS.

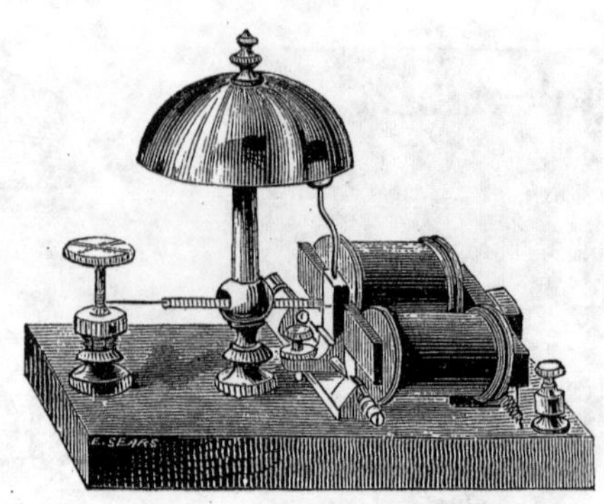

Iron Frame Wall Bells.

FINELY FINISHED.

No. 1,	with 2½ inch bell	....	$4 00
" 2,	" 3½ " "	....	4 50
" 3,	" 4 " "	....	5 25
" 4,	" 5 " "	....	6 00
" 5,	" 6 " "	....	7 00
" 6,	" 7 " "	....	7 50
" 7,	" 8 " "	....	9 00
" 8,	" 10 " "	....	18 00
" 9,	" 12 " "	....	20 00

Table or Bracket Bells.

MOUNTED ON FINELY FINISHED ROSEWOOD BASES.

No. 1,	with 2½ inch bell	....	$6 00
" 2,	" 3½ " "	....	7 00
" 3,	" 4 " "	....	8 00
" 4,	" 5 " "	....	9 00
" 5,	" 6 " "	....	10 00

Electro-Mechanical Gongs,

WITH SPRING MOVEMENT.

8 inch Gong	....	$28 00
10 " "	....	30 00
12 " "	....	35 00
14 " "	....	40 00

Liberal Discount to the Trade.

PRESS BUTTON.

[FULL SIZE.]
Finely finished Mahogany, Ash, Oak, Walnut or Rosewood.

PEAR SHAPE PUSH BUTTON FOR BELL CORD.

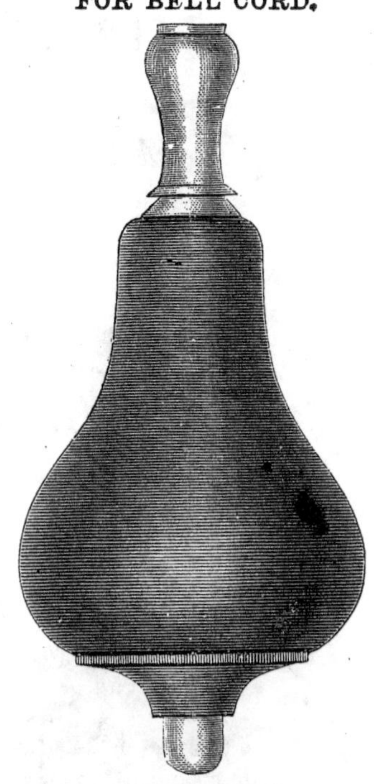

[FULL SIZE.]
Of Mahogany, Walnut or Rosewood.

PRICE LIST
—OF—
Annunciator and Burglar Alarm Material.

Push Buttons, each, Fine Finished Wood	$0 40
" " " Pear Shape	1 25
" " Porcelain, each	75
" " Bronze, "	75
" " Nickel plated, plain	75
" " " " fancy	1 00
" " For Office Desks	75
Burglar Alarm Door Springs	40
" " Window "	30
Front Door Pulls	$3 50 and 6 50
Annunciator Wire, per lb. (200 feet.)	70

Liberal Discount to the Trade.

DEEP SEA CABLES.

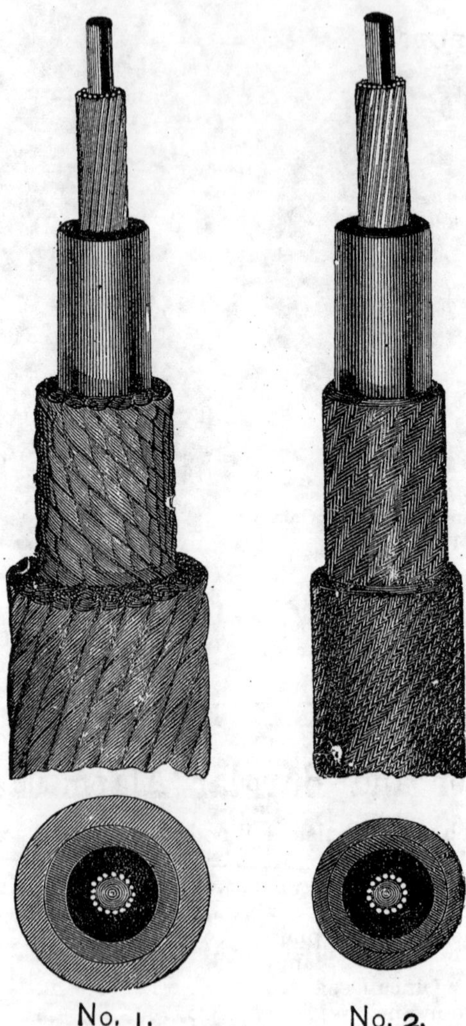

No. 1. No. 2.

SIDE AND END VIEW OF CABLES.

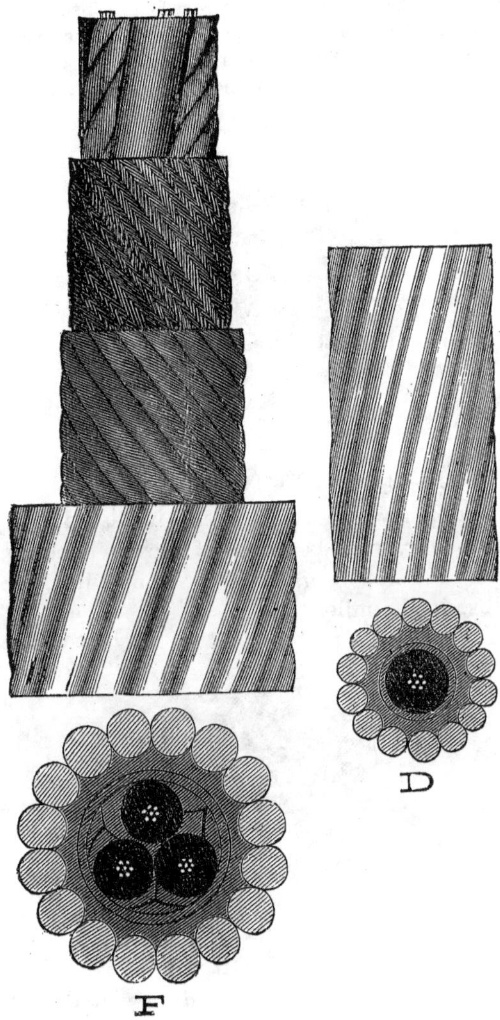

SUB-MARINE CABLES.

Manufactured under LETTERS PATENT of the United States, No. 65,019, dated May 21, 1867, granted to George B. Simpson, and now owned by Clinton G. Colgate, for the use of GUTTA PERCHA as a covering or insulator of wires for atmospheric or sub-marine telegraphic communications or for other electrical purposes.

The VALIDITY of this PATENT has been established by a decree made by the Circuit Court of the United States, held in the City of New York, dated December 8, 1878.

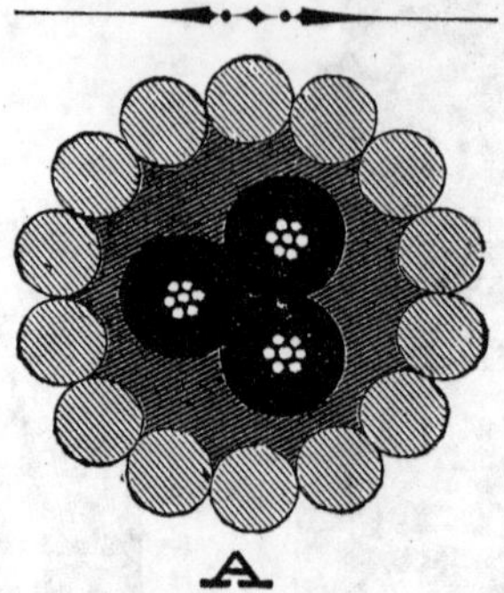

A

A—3-CONDUCTOR CABLE.

Each 7 No. 19 copper wires twisted, and insulated with pure gutta percha, 3-8 in. diameter, with bedding of woven banding and tarred hemp; armor of 14 No. 3 galvanized iron wires, spirally laid. Weighs 13,500 lbs. to the mile.

Price, 91c. per foot.

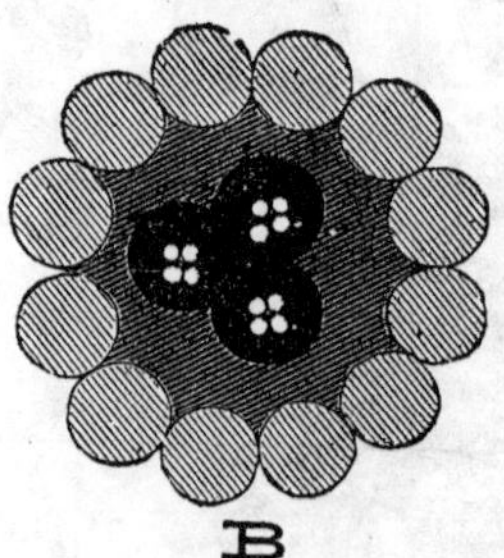

B

B—3-CONDUCTOR CABLE.

Each 4 No. 19 copper wires twisted, and insulated with pure gutta percha, 5-16 in. diameter, with bedding of woven banding and tarred hemp; armor of 12 No. 3 galvanized iron wires, spirally laid. Weighs 11,450 lbs. to the mile.

Price, 65c. per foot.

C—1-CONDUCTOR CABLE.

4 No. 19 copper wires twisted, and insulated with pure gutta percha 5-16 in. diameter, with bedding of woven banding and tarred hemp; armor of 12 No. 7 galvanized iron wires, spirally laid, Weighs 5,046 lbs. to the mile. Price, 30c. per foot.

D—1-CONDUCTOR CABLE.

7 No. 19 copper wires twisted, and insulated with pure gutta percha $\frac{3}{8}$ in. diameter, with bedding of woven banding and tarred hemp, and armor of 14 No. 7 galvanized iron wires, spirally laid. Weighs 5,850 lbs. to the mile.

Price, 38c. per foot.

E—1-CONDUCTOR CABLE.

7 No. 19 copper wires twisted, and insulated with pure gutta percha $\frac{3}{8}$ in. diameter, with bedding of woven banding, tarred, and armor of 15 No. 9 galvanized iron wires, spirally laid. Weighs 3, 550 lbs. to the mile.

Price, 35c. per foot.

F—3-CONDUCTOR CABLE.

Each 7 No. 19 copper wires twisted, and insulated with pure gutta percha $\frac{3}{8}$ in. diameter, with bedding of woven banding and hemp tarred, and armor of 16 No. 3 galvanized iron wires, spirally laid. Weighs 15,100 lbs. to the mile.

Price, $1.00 per foot.

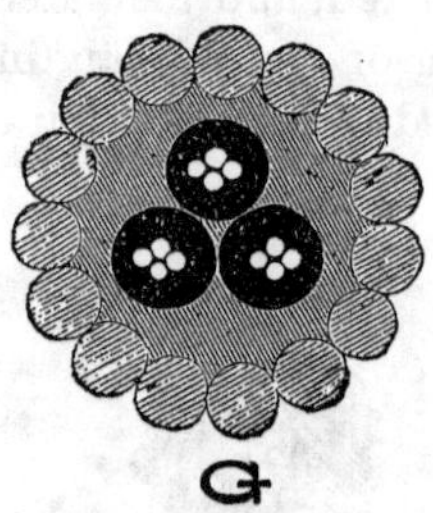

G—3-CONDUCTOR CABLE.

Each 4 No. 19 copper wires twisted, and insulated with pure gutta percha, 9-32 in. diameter, with bedding of woven banding and hemp tarred, and armor of 15 No. 5 galvanized iron wires, spirally laid. Weighs 8,170 lbs. to the mile.

Price, 51c. per foot.

H

H—1-CONDUCTOR CABLE.

7 No. 21 copper wires twisted, and insulated with pure gutta percha 9-32 in. diameter, with bedding of woven banding tarred, and armor of 10 No. 7 galvanized iron wires, spirally laid. Weighs 4,050 lbs. to the mile.

Price, 30c. per foot.

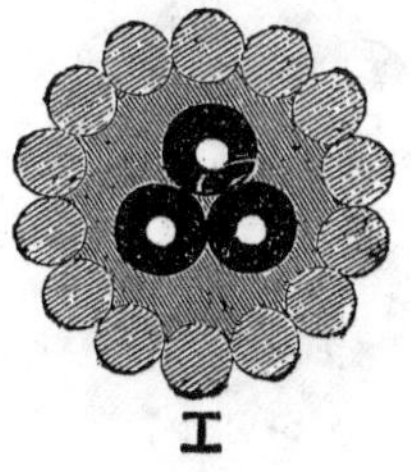

I

I—3-CONDUCTOR CABLE.

Each 1 No. 14 copper wire, and insulated with pure gutta percha, $\frac{1}{4}$ inch diameter, with bedding of woven banding and hemp tarred, and armor of 14 No. 5 galvanized iron wires, spirally laid. Weighs 8,000 pounds to the mile.

Price, 50c. per foot.

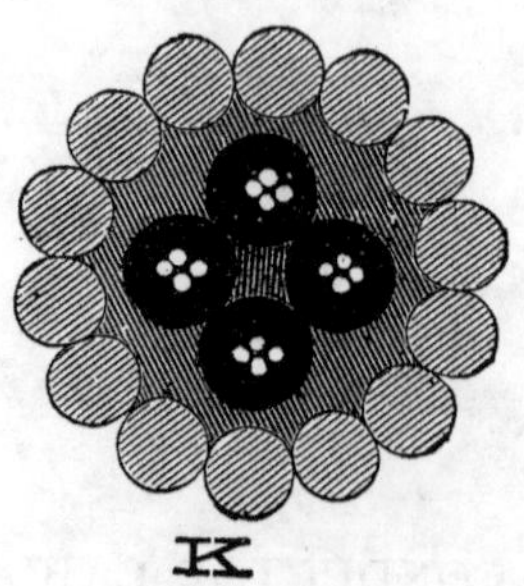

K

K—4-CONDUCTOR CABLE.

Each four No. 19 copper wires twisted, and insulated with pure gutta percha, 5-16th inch diameter, with bedding of woven banding and tarred hemp, and armor of 14 No. 3 galvanized iron wires, spirally laid. Weighs 12,715 lbs. to the mile.

Price, 88c. per foot.

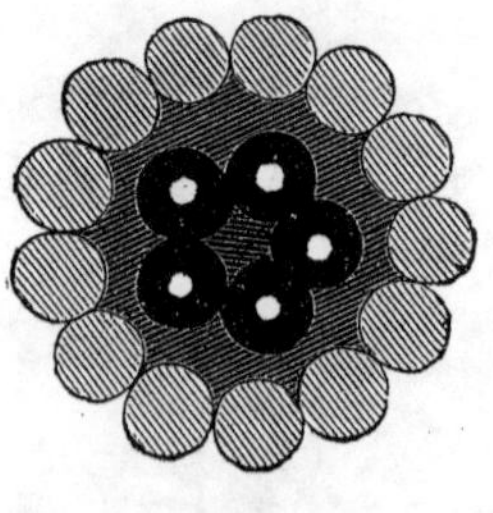

L

L—5-CONDUCTOR CABLE.

Each one No. 14 copper wire, insulated with pure gutta percha, ¼ in. diameter, with bedding of woven banding and tarred hemp, and armor of No. 3 galvanized iron wires, spirally laid. Weighs 12,000 lbs. to the mile.

Price, 80c. per foot.

M—6-CONDUCTOR CABLE.

Each 1 No. 14 copper wire, insulated with pure gutta percha, $\frac{1}{4}$ in. diameter, with bedding of woven banding and tarred hemp, and armor of 14 No. 3 galvanized iron wires, laid up spirally. Weighs 13,000 lbs. to the mile.

Price, 85c. per foot.

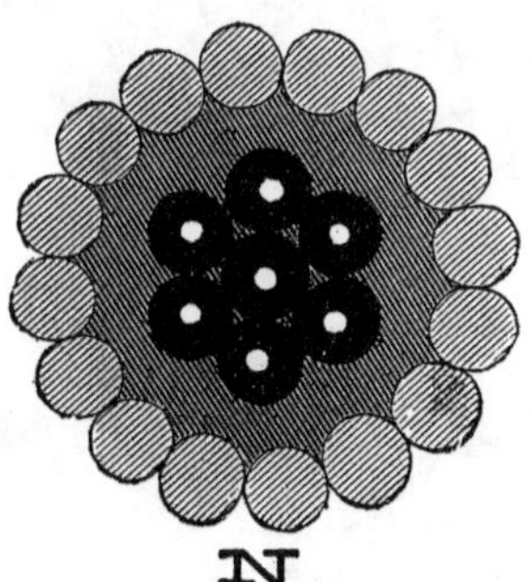

N—7-CONDUCTOR CABLE.

Each 1 No, 14 copper wire, insulated with pure gutta percha, $\frac{1}{4}$ in. diameter, with bedding of woven banding and tarred hemp, and armor of 16 No. 3 galvanized iron wires. Weighs 15,056 lbs. to the mile.

Price, $1.00 per foot.

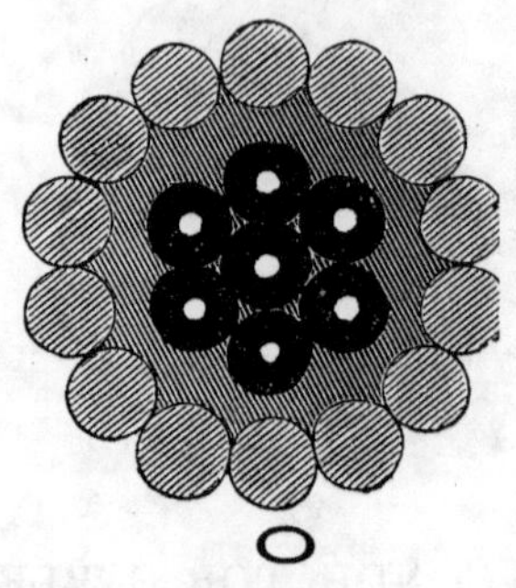

O—7-CONDUCTOR CABLE.

Each 1 No. 14 copper wire, insulated with pure gutta percha, $\frac{1}{4}$ in. diameter, with bedding of woven banding and tarred hemp, and armor of 14 No. 3 galvanized iron wires, spirally laid. Weighs 13,086 pounds to the mile.

Price, 95c. per foot.

P--1-CONDUCTOR CABLE.

1 No. 14 copper wire, insulated with pure gutta percha, $\frac{1}{4}$ in. diameter, with bedding of woven banding tarred, and armor of 12 No. 9 galvanized iron wires, spirally laid. Weighs 2,584 lbs. to the mile.

Price, 25c. per foot.

THE GAMEWELL

Fire Alarm Telegraph Company,

Nos. 5 & 7 Dey Street,

NEW YORK.

Having purchased from Messrs. Gamewell & Co., late proprietors of the "American Fire Alarm and Police Telegraph," all their patents and "good will," this Company is now prepared to contract with cities and towns for the construction of this valuable adjunct to every well-regulated Fire Department.

This system of Fire Alarm Telegraph, covered by the "Gamewell" patents, is the only **perfect**, **complete**, and **reliable** system of Fire Alarm Telegraph in the world, and the only one which has yet established its claims to perfect reliability. It is now in successful operation in over one hundred cities and towns in the United States and Canadas.

Any information desired in regard to the above system will be cheerfully and promptly furnished on application at the office.

L. G. TILLOTSON,
President.

J. N. Gamewell,
Superintendent.

Henry L. Bruns,
Secretary.

www.ingramcontent.com/pod-product-compliance
Lightning Source LLC
LaVergne TN
LVHW021403110826
845150LV00007B/1767

9781425512620